D0727522

gel Cawthorne   dred
ks, including   llers,
e Killers, Sex Killers, ~~Satanic Killers~~, Magic
ers, The Mammoth Book of Killers at Large, House
Horrors – The Horrific True Story of Josef Fritzl, the
her from Hell, The World's Ten Most Evil Men,
stralian True Crime, The World's Most Evil Gangsters,
rates of the 21st Century, Stalin's Crimes, Jack the
pper's Secret Confession and The Immortals. He lives
London.

VIGILANTES

Nigel Cawthorne

Quercus

First published in 2010 by

Quercus
21 Bloomsbury Square
London
WC1A 2NS

ISBN 978 1 84916 025 4

10 9 8 7 6 5 4 3 2 1

Typeset by Ellipsis Books Limited, Glasgow

Printed and bound in Great Britain by Clays Ltd, St Ives plc

CONTENTS

INTRODUCTION:
THE LAW OF THE JUNGLE

The word vigilante conjures up the image of a group of concerned citizens taking the law into their own hands over the head of the local sheriff or Federal marshal in the lawless West. In classic Westerns, they almost always string up the wrong man, who then has to be saved by the hero – unless the man at the end of the rope is the hero himself. Then his sidekick or the love interest steps in.

However, since the moral certainties of Hollywood in the early twentieth century have been overthrown, the vigilante has moved into centre stage. He – and it almost always is a he – has resumed the traditional role of knight-errant, the one virtuous man who single-handedly takes on the lawless world. Both Superman and Batman are vigilantes, so is the Watchman. While John McClane – the Bruce Willis figure in the *Die Hard* movies – is a New York cop, he uses decidedly extra-judicial methods when he takes on the bad guys. Working outside the law, he is essentially a vigilante.

Real-life New York boasts its own vigilantes. In 1984, seemingly mild-mannered Bernhard Goetz was surrounded by four African-American teenagers who demanded money. He pulled a .38 Smith & Wesson Special from his windcheater and shot all four of them. They survived, though one was paralysed and suffered brain damage when a bullet severed his spinal cord. Goetz was quickly dubbed the 'subway vigilante' by the newspapers. He gave himself up nine days later, but was acquitted on charges of attempted murder, assault, reckless endangerment, and several gun crimes. A Manhattan jury found him guilty only of the possession of an illegal firearm. He served two-thirds of a one-year sentence.

In June 2009, two alleged rapists were beaten by mobs in the streets of Philadelphia, the city of brotherly love. Members of the Minuteman Civil Defense Corps – an anti-immigration vigilante group – were charged with a double homicide and one count of attempted murder in Arizona. Four men were indicted for passing themselves off as federal agents to recover money from three hedge-fund managers linked to a Ponzi scheme. Three men were jailed for meting out vigilante justice to two others who were trying to steal scrap metal from their father's plant. An alleged cop killer was strangled in custody and no one was charged.

VIGILANTES

A vigilante pumped five bullets into a robber he had shot and immobilised minutes earlier as he lay on the floor of an Oklahoma City pharmacy, killing the sixteen-year-old. A pro-life killer gunned down an abortionist in Wichita, Kansas ...

But these are Americans. Surely the British don't go around taking the law into their own hands? Oh, but they do. Sometimes their illegal actions have a political motivation. Animal rights activists are only too keen to break into farms and laboratories where they believe animals are being subjected to cruelty. Extremists have issued threats against researchers. Some have even resorted to arson and criminal damage.

Other political activists, convinced of the rightness of their cause, also see themselves above the law. They assault politicians with eggs, custard pies and, in one case, green custard, and they have smashed the windows of banks.

In Hampshire in 2006, a vigilante launched a campaign against those using a mobile phone while driving a car, which was made a criminal offence in the UK in December 2003. More than twenty car owners had their tyres slashed. A note using words cut from newspapers was left on their windscreens. It read: 'Warning, you have been seen while using your mobile phone.'

One victim, Rebecca Rendle, was left with a £170 bill when all four of her tyres were punctured outside her Gosport home.

'I was shocked and furious – I don't even own a mobile,' she said. Someone must have followed her home 'as that's the only way they would find out where you live. There's a loony who thinks they are doing the world a favour.'

As so often, the vigilante had attacked the wrong person.

The British are most likely to take the law into their own hands when it comes to paedophiles – or suspected paedophiles. In 1997, one senior policeman described the increasing number of mob attacks as 'justice by the law of the jungle'. John Evans, Chief Constable of Devon and Cornwall, said: 'The vigilante action we have seen has not only been improper and unlawful, but there is also a danger that we will drive the real paedophiles underground.'

Since then, things have got worse. With the *News of the World* name-and-shame campaign in 2000, mobs took to the street in the Paulsgrove area of Portsmouth. The innocent and the guilty alike were attacked. When an innocent man who was mistaken for a convicted paedophile named and shamed in the *Manchester Evening News* was attacked and seriously injured, the editor said he took no responsibility for the action. However, the *News of the World*'s editor Rebekah Wade saw sense and stopped her newspaper's campaign.

While demonstrations and vigilante attacks have driven from their homes paedophiles who might be a danger to local children, other entirely innocent people have been targeted as well. Some vigilantes are not even content with forcing sex offenders out of their neighbourhoods: they sometimes take it upon themselves to impose the death penalty on their victims, a practice abandoned by the law a long time ago. Again, as a result, innocent people have been killed.

A father of six was stabbed nineteen times by three brothers in Camberwell in revenge for an attack he had no connection with. He bled to death and they were convicted of murder. In Scotland, a man was driven out of his home town by vigilantes after he had been falsely accused of rape. While in Liverpool, a sixteen-year-old shot a drug-dealer for threatening his mentally ill mother. He got seven years. And there are more such cases.

I must admit that when I was asked to write a book about vigilantes in the Underworld UK series, I thought it would be impossible. Apart from the well-publicised incidents, I imagined that the British were far too level-headed to resort to mob rule. I was wrong. Searching through the newspaper archives, I discovered that the country is suffering an epidemic of rough justice. It appears that people no longer have faith in the police and the courts to deal with criminals appropriately. Or maybe they are just too impatient. If a perceived wrong has been done, they want it righted immediately. They do not want to wait for due process as the machinery of justice grinds awfully slowly.

Although we all know that we should not take the law into our own hands, there is right and wrong on both sides here. Some people had been attacked and had their property vandalised with scant protection offered by the police. They have been threatened, abused and assaulted beyond endurance – and finally snapped. Fortunately, in most cases, while they have suffered the inconvenience of protracted court hearings, they have been exonerated in the end.

While it is easy in many cases to sympathise with those who have taken the law into their own hands, we all live a small step from anarchy. Once the mob takes the streets, only the strong survive. Only too quickly the guiltless – such as you and me – can find themselves dangling from the end of a rope, like in those old cowboy movies. There have been no lynchings in this country recently. That, in itself, is surprising. Looking beneath the UK's underbelly you will see how close we have come.

Nigel Cawthorne
Bloomsbury, July 2009

CHAPTER 1
THE MERSTHAM MOB

In January 2009, a mob of vigilantes wearing bala-clavas took to the streets of the Surrey village of Merstham, which lies in the midst of the stockbroker belt. One of them was wielding a machete. They were members of the self-styled Merstham Justice Squad that was formed after young women were pursued by a suspected sex attacker in Merstham and nearby Redhill on 30 December 2008. A nineteen-year-old was raped in Gatton Park Road, Redhill, the previous May. No one had been arrested in connection with these crimes.

'We all know one of the girls who was attacked,' the vigilantes' leader said. 'We didn't want our wives, sisters and daughters falling prey to this beast, so we decided to go out there as a visible presence to scare him off and hopefully even catch him. We were also on the lookout for any burglars or anyone else posing a threat. We think the police are too concerned about catching kids smoking cannabis and drinking when they should be concentrating on the real criminals.'

The gang, which comprised thirty men aged between eighteen and thirty, said that their presence on the street of the village made the residents feel safe. They also claimed to be offering reward money for information about the incidents to members of the community.

'It's time for the community to stand up for itself and do something,' said a spokesman, who refused to be identified. 'This area has really gone downhill in the last year and we feel we need to sort out the problems ourselves.'

The vigilantes said they would detain and give an 'army style' interrogation to any suspects they 'caught in the act'. Kangaroo courts would be set up and summary justice dispensed.

'It's the older guys who will make up the panel who judge anyone we catch,' said a younger member. 'They are sensible, law-abiding people and they will be fair. We are not a lynch mob.'

If a suspect was found guilty, the vigilante tribunal would hand down its punishment, he said.

In response, Detective Inspector Juliet Parker of the Surrey Police said: 'The force will take a zero-tolerance stance against anyone who decides to take the law into their own hands and we will prosecute offenders to the fullest extent of the law. Instead members of the community are encouraged to work with detectives at Surrey Police to help identify and catch this man.'

A team of officers was working on Operation Speedbird investigating the suspicious incidents in Merstham and Redhill and witness appeals had been issued on 31 December and 9 January.

The anonymous spokesman for the vigilantes said that they would be happy to cooperate with the police.

'We want to do right and not wrong,' he said. 'We are happy to work with the police to help catch whoever is chasing women.'

Nevertheless, the police took a dim view of the group's activities after they posed for a photograph that appeared in the local paper – and was then picked up nationally. In it, the *Daily Mail* pointed out, the balaclavaed vigilantes looked more like Northern Irish paramilitaries than Neighbourhood Watch.

Surrey's Divisional Commander, Chief Superintendent Adrian Harper made it clear in no uncertain terms that vigilantes were not welcome in the area.

'It is my responsibility, and that of my many officers, to ensure those who live in east Surrey are safe and feel safe,' he said, 'and I cannot emphasise enough how irresponsible it is for people to take the law into their own hands. I will deal robustly with anyone who does resort to vigilantism and targets who they believe may be responsible for these incidents. Often "justice" groups target the wrong person and an innocent member of the community is seriously injured, something which is neither just nor fair.'

As part of their zero-tolerance stance the police hunted down the leader of the Merstham Justice Squad. Though masked, he had been identified from the picture on the front page of the *Surrey Mirror*; he handed himself in at Reigate police station after officers visited his house. Later, the machete was handed in and the leader had a face-to-face meeting with Chief Superintendent Harper.

Afterwards, the man, who would not be named, said: 'I guess a few of the guys got a bit carried away. We have ditched the balaclavas and handed in the machete. But loads of people support what we are doing. They say they feel safer with us out there because they don't see enough police walking the beat.'

Navigor – the National Vigilante Organisation – took issue with Chief Superintendent Harper, saying that it was neither 'just nor fair' that decent people had to resort to vigilantism because of 'New Labour's "protect-a-thug" mentality.'

'Nor is it "just or fair" that many police forces prefer chasing those who stand up to the thugs rather than dealing with the thugs properly,' Navigor said. 'Until we get real justice for real crimes and end the criminalisation of ordinary people, actions like this will simply increase. And when Chief Superintendent Adrian Harper says: "It is my responsibility, and that of my many officers, to ensure those who live in east Surrey are safe and feel safe" perhaps he should ask himself "why are we failing so badly" and why do people feel so unsafe that they have to form a vigilante group to protect themselves? And when he says "how irresponsible it is for people to take the law into their own hands", perhaps he should ask himself "What law?" A law which prosecutes decent people for protecting themselves?'

The organisation drew attention to the cases of people like Stephan Toth, Paul Lawson and Steve Kink. All three suffered after confronting law-breakers themselves.

Stephan Toth took action when a thirteen-year-old boy hurled threats and abuse through an open window at his wife Selina, who was suffering from cancer. The 34-year-old father said: 'I went up to him and said, "Enough is enough".'

The boy responded, 'You can't touch me, I'll get you sacked.'

'I thought his mum should hear this,' said Toth, 'so with open palms I coaxed him towards her house, which is a few doors down. My job is providing support and care at a school for children with learning and physical disabilities, so I've been trained on how to handle youths properly and barely even touched his shoulders.'

But the boy claimed Mr Toth grabbed him in a bear hug and tried to pick him up, causing six scratches to his chest. He broke free and ran off. When Mr Toth told the boy's mother what her son had done, she refused to believe a word of it, so he called the police and left them to deal with it. But half an hour later the police came around and arrested him, after the boy's family lodged a complaint.

Toth found himself detained in a filthy cell for eight hours before facing a two-hour interrogation. Then he was charged with common assault. Three months later, he appeared before the magistrates in Margate.

'There is insufficient evidence that there was a bear hug causing injuries but the defendant has admitted that he took hold of him by his shoulders and that constitutes an assault in our opinion,' said Tony Pomeroy, chairman of the bench. 'We think, however, that there was some degree of provocation in this.'

Nevertheless, Toth was convicted.

Pomeroy added: 'It would be an idea next time just to walk away.'

Toth had to pay £85 costs, but otherwise was given an absolute discharge. However, the conviction left him with a criminal record as a convicted vigilante and he lost his job as a carer.

'I've been treated appallingly,' he said. 'My career is

looking like it's going to be crushed, we have bills to pay and my wife's already fragile health is worse because of this.'

Kent Crown Prosecution Service defended its decision to take Mr Toth to court. A spokesman said: 'The CPS only brings a prosecution if there is enough evidence to provide a reasonable chance of conviction and if the prosecution is in the public interest.'

Retired Metropolitan police officer Paul Lawson got out of his car to confront youths when they threw a beer can at him in Morpeth outside Newcastle-upon-Tyne. He planned to make a citizen's arrest, but when the thugs surrounded him and threatened to kill him and smash up his vehicle he backed down.

'They were the usual crowd of boy racers who gather in Morpeth,' he said. 'I got out and moved towards them. I was going to make a citizen's arrest, but things very quickly turned nasty. I was surrounded by about twelve of them. They told me to leave or they would kill me and the ringleader said if he saw my car parked in Morpeth again they would wreck it.'

Instead of taking the law into his own hands, ex-Inspector Lawson reported the incident to two police officers on patrol in the area. However, they refused to take action and Lawson found himself under arrest when one of the gang claimed to have been assaulted by him.

NIGEL CAWTHORNE

Even though the patrolling officers hadn't bothered to take the former Metropolitan inspector's details, once the thugs made a complaint they were able to trace Lawson through his car's registration number. He was asked to attend Bedlington police station, where he was held in a cell for two hours. He was then interviewed and arrested on suspicion of assault causing bodily harm, and had his fingerprints and a DNA sample taken.

'The police refused my solicitor's request that there was clearly no need for further action, and I was released on bail,' he said.

After a delay of seven weeks, a decision was made to take no further action against him, and he got a call saying there was no case to answer.

'I have not heard about any action taken against the youths who threatened me,' said Lawson. 'I am still waiting for my allegations to be investigated and I am very angry about the whole experience. After thirty years of serving as a policeman and upholding the Queen's peace, I could have acted as a professional witness and perhaps got rid of yobs who at times are the scourge of Morpeth.'

However, as he was no longer a policeman, his action was considered vigilante.

He is furious that the yobs who threatened him have never been brought to justice and described the actions of Northumbria Police as an 'utter disgrace'.

Ironically, before he retired to his native Northumberland after thirty years in the Met, Paul Lawson headed the Professional Standards Unit and his job involved investigating the professional conduct of police officers.

'I still can't believe this,' he said of the actions of the Northumbria Police. 'At the time this happened, I was distraught going through the whole process, bearing in mind the background I come from. As far as I am concerned, they just abrogated their responsibility and should be ashamed of themselves.'

Chief Inspector John Barnes, of the Northumbria Police Northumberland Area Command, said: 'Anyone who feels unhappy with the way they have been treated by Northumbria Police can always make use of our official complaints procedure.'

Steve Kink apprehended a thug after catching him breaking into a mobile phone shop late at night. However, as the police do not like people who take the law into their own hands he was charged with assault, even though he was attacked by the thug and punched in the face.

The 47-year-old businessman was in his wife's bar, Jakes, above the Colwell shopping centre in Weymouth, Dorset, after midnight when he heard the sound of a security alarm coming from downstairs. Even though he was registered disabled after a motorcycle accident twenty years before, Kink, who owns the Ink Fever tattoo parlour in the Colwell centre, went downstairs and confronted two men outside the Phone Zone store whose window they had just smashed. He was met with a volley of abuse. Then one of the men attacked him, punching him in the face and causing a cut under his eye.

'The yob took a swing at me and punched me just under my left eye,' said Kink. 'I grabbed hold of him and managed to sweep one of his legs from under him.'

Despite the punch in the face, he managed to pin the offender to the floor. The other man made off. Passers-by called the police and Toth held on to the 25-year-old until officers arrived. At the time, they praised him for his efforts and arrested the man on suspicion of criminal damage. However, at the police station, the offender was let off with a caution.

Four days later, three police officers and a dog-handler turned up at Kink's house to arrest him.

'They told me I was being arrested for assault,' he said. 'But I didn't know what they were talking about at first … The allegation is that I poked this guy in the eyes. I deny this and have fifteen or sixteen witnesses to back me up.'

Kink was taken to the local police station where he was held in a cell for six hours before being questioned. Then he was charged with grievous bodily harm, a charge that can bring up to six years in jail.

He was appalled at the way he was treated. He said: 'I thought I was doing the right thing by making a bit of a citizen's arrest. All I did was use reasonable force to hold him down. It makes you think and it puts me off trying to get involved in something like that again ... Now this fuss with the police has put me off helping, but I'm not sure I can live with myself if I see an old lady mugged and I just walk on by.'

The boss of the Phone Zone store the men had tried to burgle said: 'I am grateful to Steve. He did the job that the police are supposed to do. The damage to the window was £250 but I don't know how and when I am going to get that back.'

Tory MP Philip Davies described the case as outrageous and said it was a sad indictment of the state of the criminal justice system.

'This is quite simply ridiculous,' said the MP. 'People who are prepared to put themselves in danger to apprehend criminals ought to be rewarded, not punished.'

Four months later Steve Kink was acquitted by Weymouth magistrates.

'It's a huge weight off my mind,' he said. 'But it has left a bitter taste in the mouth.'

Despite widespread support for the vigilante action of

Steve Kink and others, the *Sun* took issue with the Merstham vigilantes.

'This cannot and must not be the way forward,' the paper said. 'But what is the police answer to rising crime across Britain? Cardboard coppers. Thirteen forces have spent £20,000 on flatpack bobbies which are propped up in doorways and petrol stations. West Midlands alone has ordered eighty cardboard constables. That's the way to keep the streets safe!'

However, the emergence of Merstham Justice Squad seemed to have done some good. After the Squad doffed their balaclavas, a spokesman said: 'There's definitely more police around at the moment, but all they seem to be doing is stopping kids in the street. Obviously, with all the police here now we're not going to go around the streets in balaclavas, but we are still asking around [about the prowler]. From speaking to people it's clear there's a lot of support for us and what we are trying to do.'

The gang met up after their appearance in the newspapers and had a number of meetings to talk about the most appropriate ways to deal with the situation. They reaffirmed that they were happy to work with police and share information.

The spokesman added: 'We're not giving up, we have suspicions about people and we are watching them.'

A Surrey Police spokesman said: 'Police presence in the area is to reassure the community and to carry out patrols as a result of the two incidents. Anyone who has their suspicions should pass on that information to Surrey Police and not take matters into their own hands.'

CHAPTER 2
KIDNAPPING

Fifty-seven-year-old Frank McCourt took the law into his own hands and made a citizen's arrest on a yob terrorising his home, but was then arrested himself – on suspicion of kidnapping. He faced a three-month legal ordeal while the boy and his gang went unpunished.

The story began on 17 February 2008 when a pack of youths hurled sticks, stones, mud and eggs at houses in Crawley, West Sussex. McCourt and his wife Maria had just sat down to dinner when they heard a bang on the front window. Their house came under attack from two boys aged about ten or eleven. McCourt, a former soldier who had seen service in Northern Ireland and Somalia, went out to confront them.

'I opened the door and shouted: "What do you think you are doing?"' he said.

'Fuck off, Grandad,' came the sharp retort.

'They called me an effing B, an effing C,' said McCourt. Then one of the boys ran at Frank and kicked him, while the other continued bombard his home.

'They were cursing and swearing like I've never heard,' he said. 'I managed to catch one of them by the arm, but he started to kick me in the legs.'

His assailant fell in the bushes. As McCourt went to pick him up, his wife came outside and told him that it was best to leave the matter to the police.

'So I let the kid go and told them never to come back here again,' McCourt said.

However, when he came back from his job – delivering and fitting oxygen masks for the seriously ill – the following day, he found his wife in tears. All afternoon she had suffered abuse from the gang who had pelted the house with missiles once again.

'She was absolutely terrified,' he said. 'She told me a gang of kids had been throwing things at the house all afternoon, and shouting all the names under the sun at her.'

'While Frank was out at work, the boys came back with reinforcements,' said Maria, a clerk for a national courier company. 'I left the house to walk the dogs and this time there was seven or eight of them.'

Among them were the two boys from the previous night.

'I'm not confrontational so I stuck my nose in the air and walked to the end of the road,' she said. 'I could see they were following me and getting closer. They were calling my dogs "rats", poking them with sticks and saying they should be put down. I said, "Leave me alone", rushed inside and phoned Frank. He could hear in my voice that I was upset, which is not like me at all.'

'She could barely talk for crying,' said McCourt. 'When I got home, she told me she had gone to walk the dogs. The two kids from the night before had come up behind her with about six others. They were prodding the dogs with sticks and saying they were going to kill them. The dogs were terrified. So was Maria.'

Within an hour of his return, they were back throwing sticks, stones, mud and eggs at the McCourts' £170,000 semi-detached home. McCourt shepherded his wife into his car as the youths hurled abuse from the end of the street, and drove her to her afternoon shift at work.

'They were still there when I returned, throwing whatever they could get their hands on,' he said. 'They put me through two hours of hell.'

McCourt called a police antisocial behaviour hotline, but was kept on hold for three-quarters of an hour.

'I didn't call 999 because I didn't think it was a big enough incident,' he said. 'I didn't want to upset the emergency services.' After all, during his twelve years' service in the army, he had seen children of the same age armed with knives, petrol bombs and machine guns.

The bombardment continued while McCourt was left

hanging on on the so-called hotline. 'It just rang for forty-five minutes,' he said. 'No answer, no hold music, no "Greensleeves".'

So he went out to look for a policeman, but found none.

'I gave up trying to ring the police, and took a walk round the corner to see if I could find a community bobby on the beat,' said McCourt. 'But, of course, there wasn't one. Meanwhile, those kids were outside terrorising my house ... By this time, we'd put up with three hours of being terrorised in our own home. The kids were still trying to smash our windows, but I wasn't having it any more.'

With no sign of the police, McCourt had no alternative. Exploiting a lull, he slipped out of his house and round the corner.

'The two ten-year-olds were beating a waste bin with sticks. I got one of them by the front of his shirt. I didn't hurt him. I just told him, "You are under citizen's arrest."'

Then McCourt marched the foul-mouthed youngster back with him to his house.

'I told him: "I am not going to harm you, but I want to contact your family and the police."'

The boy said he was asthmatic and asked for an aspirin.

'Of course I fetched a tablet,' said McCourt.

He demanded the boy's name and his mother's phone

number. But while he was trying to call her, she was called by another member of the gang. She raced to the McCourts' home and began banging on the door, shouting and swearing.

'I offered to explain, but she was swearing as badly as her son,' McCourt said. 'The language from that woman was absolutely unbelievable. Now I know where the kids get it from. She said she didn't want me manhandling her son. I said if she'd brought him up properly, I wouldn't have to.'

Frank McCourt was doubly appalled by the mother's attitude because, thirty years before, his young son Mark was accused of throwing a stone at a car. The driver had frogmarched the boy home and told McCourt what the six-year-old had done. Frank, then 27, immediately apologised for the boy's behaviour and chastised him with a smack on the legs.

The following day his wife Maria took Mark around to the driver's house so he could apologise again for his behaviour.

'Mark has always insisted that it was his friend who had actually thrown the stone but he's never been in trouble from that day to this,' said Maria, thirty years later. 'He knows that his father is a real stickler for good behaviour.'

When the McCourts' house came under bombardment from a group of feral eleven-year-olds throwing stones and eggs – and he actually caught one of them red-handed – the former soldier received no such apologies. Not only that, he got further abuse. When he let the boy go, he walked over to his mother 'calling me an effing C,' said McCourt. He even invited her inside to discuss the problem.

'All I wanted her to do was apologise,' he said.

But, minutes later, the police turned up.

'You know what?' said McCourt. 'I even thanked them for coming.'

The officers spoke to McCourt, then to the boys.

Then they said, 'There's been a serious allegation. We must investigate. We are arresting you for kidnapping.'

'I thought they were joking,' said McCourt.

The police took him to Crawley police station to be bailed, then drove him home to a wife who was in floods of tears once again. Meanwhile, no action was taken against the gang of youths that attacked his home. They were sent home without so much as a telling off, McCourt complained.

'Even though the boys admitted everything, I was still charged, while they have been given a green light to continue their despicable behaviour,' he said. 'It's utterly disgraceful that something like this can happen in this day and age. Gangs of hooligans who are barely out of short trousers can roam the streets unchecked, causing misery for entire neighbourhoods – and if you try and stand in their way, you end up in the dock.'

At first, some of the police officers were sympathetic, McCourt said.

'One said, "If it had been me, I would have slapped him."'

They told McCourt that the kids concerned were known to the police. They reassured him the charges were 'nothing, rubbish.'

'Of course I believed them. I thought the case was bound to be dropped.'

McCourt spent six weeks on bail. Then, when he answered bail for a second time on 3 April 2008, police said they would let him off with a caution. McCourt refused to accept that, saying to do so would be an admission of guilt. The police then charged him with the lesser offence of assault, but he still faced a jail sentence of up to six months.

'They searched me, took my shoes away,' he said. 'They took DNA samples. They put me in a cell for two hours. I wasn't frightened. I was angry.'

Former Home Secretary Ann Widdecombe said: 'It tells you everything that is wrong in Britain today. Police operate according to political correctness, and not common sense.'

She was joined in her attack by Tory MP Philip Davies, who said: 'The whole of the law is there on the side of thugs and yobs and totally against decent, law-abiding members of the public. Until we get a criminal justice system that protects decent people and clamps down hard on these yobs, we're never going to make any headway. The police should apologise to this gentleman and instead bring these thugs to justice.'

McCourt appeared before magistrates and the trial date was set for 20 June 2008 in Haywards Heath. Afterwards he found he could not sleep and turned to drink, until, he said, 'I realised I couldn't hide behind the bottle.'

A fortnight after his first court appearance, dog excrement was smeared on his van, but again the police were of little help.

'When I phoned, they said: "We'll give you a crime number." That was it,' he said.

The intimidation continued with a night-time visit from men challenging him to a fight.

'One drove almost to the front door with the headlights on full beam,' McCourt said. 'Two jumped out and said, "Come out and be a man."'

McCourt was tempted, but realised that discretion was the better part of valour. 'I was on bail,' he said. 'If I went to defend myself, I would be in trouble.'

This time the police did at least turn up – long after the men had left.

'Three and a half hours later, two constables arrived,' he said. 'They asked if I had seen the registration numbers. I explained I was blinded by the headlights. They said: "There's nothing we can do."'

McCourt's wife grew worried that they might be attacked again. While Frank had been accused of taking vigilante action, he was now the target of it himself.

'I wondered what would happen next,' she said. 'I backed Frank all the way, but subconsciously I was thinking, "Why couldn't you have just let them carry on throwing stones?"'

Her GP prescribed antidepressants. This helped her nerves, but she still had little faith in the police to defend her husband.

'They are extremely nice to your face,' she said. 'Then they look around and think, "Who's the easiest one to charge?" We call it back-to-front Britain: the hard-working, honest people are sent to the back. The yobs go to the front of the queue.'

Then two days before the hearing he was told the case had been dropped after his wife contacted their MP, Laura Moffat. She took the matter up with police and, in just four days, she managed to persuade the Crown Prosecution Service that there was no realistic prospect of a conviction and pursuing the case was 'not in the public interest'. Although they did not go ahead, McCourt's fingerprints and a sample of his DNA will remain on file.

'They dragged me through the courts while doing everything to protect those kids who terrorised my neighbourhood,' said McCourt. 'They were even going to give evidence in court via video-link to protect them from having to go into the court-room.'

He was adamant: 'If they're old enough to destroy people's houses, they're old enough to go to court. They should all be sent to Borstal, and their parents with them. The British criminal justice system is a laughing stock. Cases like mine must be highlighted, so people can see how stupid it is.'

After the case was dropped, Ann Widdecombe said: 'The real issue in this case is that Mr McCourt had to wait forty-five minutes on a telephone hotline, while the mother got the police there immediately.'

Laura Moffat, Labour MP for Crawley, said the family had been terrorised by yobs who made their lives a misery.

'Thankfully, common sense won the day,' she said. 'This family has suffered an horrendous level of intimidation from antisocial youths, who have thrown stones at their house, threatened to kill their dogs, and basically made their lives a misery. I just wanted the police and CPS to see sense. There was a reason why Mr McCourt performed a citizen's arrest – it's because he was at his wits' end.'

Sussex Police would not discuss the case, but a spokesman said: 'An allegation was made to police and officers duly investigated. A file was presented to the Crown Prosecution Service in accordance with procedure.'

McCourt was particularly incensed that no action was taken against the boys.

'Those children have got away scot-free,' he said. 'They are the criminals of the future and they've been given the green light to carry on as they were, while I've been put through three months of hell. This country is going to the dogs and its justice system is a joke … Britain is a place where normal people get disciplined and gangs walk free. These street gangs are allowed to do what they want while being protected by political correctness – parents and schools are now too scared to discipline them. But the police and the government aren't doing anything to protect the communities they are destroying. When we were growing up, this would never have happened. I fought for my country but now I've lost all my respect for it.'

His wife Maria bemoans his loss of patriotism and, though they had been lifelong Labour supporters, they intended to vote Conservative at the next election.

When their story appeared in the *Daily Express*, the newspaper received hundreds of letters and phone calls in support of McCourt's action. His neighbours considered him a hero. They had been preparing placards and planned to demonstrate outside the court when he went to trial. The police, they maintained, were of little use against the antisocial behaviour they had suffered.

Meanwhile Frank McCourt was unabashed.

'They picked the wrong man and the wrong house,'

he said. 'I was simply doing the job that the police should have been doing.'

Although his action nearly cost him his liberty, he did not regret it. 'I would do 110 per cent the same thing again,' he said.

McCourt's determination to stand up against the boys who sought to break his windows and intimidate his wife without apparent rebuke from their parents was all the more understandable when you consider his own upbringing. A former Barnardo's boy, he never knew either of his parents. He was fostered by a strict couple who were liberal with corporal punishment. Beaten by his foster father, a master-of-hounds, he left the Republic of Ireland at fifteen, never to return.

'Although he was a hard man, I still respected him,' said McCourt. 'And, after an upbringing like that, I certainly knew what was right and what was wrong.'

He arrived in Liverpool with just a carrier bag. He could not read or write and was forced to live rough until, at the age of sixteen, he joined the British army. There he was taught to read and write and the army gave him the determination to make something of himself.

'I've worked hard all my life,' said McCourt. 'I've never been on the dole. I have never had a criminal record.'

His only son Mark works with mentally handicapped children and had followed the excellent example of his father with his own children, aged six and seven.

'I own my house,' said McCourt. 'Every penny I've earned has gone into it and four years ago I paid off the mortgage. I've worked overtime to put in a new driveway and I've even managed to earn the money for a conservatory.'

So, when some badly brought-up boys attacked his home he was prepared to defend by any means necessary. He was particularly outraged when, rather than arrest the boys responsible for the attack, the police asked: 'Why don't you move house?'

'But why should I move?' said McCourt. 'I've worked all my life for this.'

However, the McCourts had reason to be optimistic. Maria was starting up a Neighbourhood Watch scheme. 'I am not letting our streets deteriorate any further,' she said.

Eventually, the police were forced to apologise. Chief Superintendent Wayne Jones, of Sussex Police, and Chief Inspector Jim Read, the Crawley District Commander, visited the McCourts to say sorry face-to-face.

'I have been demanding that kind of visit since the incident in February,' said McCourt, adding wryly, 'It has only taken four months.'

He complained that the officers still warned him that the youngsters who attacked him were juveniles whose identity could not be disclosed. 'The law is still protecting them. Why?'

The senior police officers had no answer. However,

Chief Superintendent Jones said: 'Mr and Mrs McCourt were pleased that we were prepared to apologise and are very keen to work with us to develop a Neighbourhood Watch Scheme in the area. We will always give priority to incidents where families or individuals are being targeted repeatedly. Anyone who forcibly takes a child into their own home against the child's will is, to say the least, likely to be closely questioned about their action. Nevertheless, following the decision not to proceed with a criminal prosecution for assault, it is right that Sussex Police expresses its sincere regret for the distress caused to Mr McCourt during the period the threat of prosecution was hanging over him.'

McCourt was somewhat less than delighted.

'I am very happy the police have taken this on the chin and apologised,' he said. 'But the whole thing was a disgrace from start to finish. They arrested the wrong man.'

Meanwhile Sussex Police issued a statement saying: 'Our neighbourhood teams are engaged with the families to address the issue of antisocial behaviour ... Sussex Police expresses its sincere regret for the distress caused.' However, the statement went on to say: 'The attending officers, faced with the alleged facts, made the correct decision to arrest and continue the investigation. Anyone who forcibly takes a child against their will is likely to be questioned.'

Frank McCourt was disillusioned. 'A little bit of me

has been destroyed for ever,' he said. 'The bit that believed in British justice, that thought I would get help when I needed it, instead of being betrayed.'

The whole affair left the McCourts with scars, mental and marital, that would not heal.

'I have worked all my life to get this home, in this street, which I love,' said Mr McCourt. 'Even if it means prison, I would do it all again to protect my home and family.'

However, his wife was not so resolute.

'If I had to go through that again,' said Maria, 'I would walk out. I back Frank, but I just couldn't face it again … We have been left defenceless.'

CHAPTER 3
HAVE-A-GO HEROES

Sometimes a vigilante who takes the law into their own hands is praised as a 'have-go-hero'. That's what happened to Thomas Delaney who kicked a thug in the head to stop him stabbing a teenager and very likely murdering him. Judge Clement Goldstone, QC, at Manchester Crown court urged the police to reward Delaney for his courage and he was recommended for a bravery award.

Delaney was driving home from work through Mossley, Greater Manchester, on 27 September 2008 when he spotting two thugs – 22-year-old Richard Hill and his accomplice nineteen-year-old Daniel Livesley – attacking seventeen-year-old Christopher Pourabolghassiam. Christopher had been at a bus stop on Egmont Street with a sixteen-year-old pal when they became embroiled in an argument with a man who turned out to be a friend of Hill and Livesley. During the altercation, the unidentified man warned them that he would get them 'battered'. As the boys left the bus stop, the man shouted: 'Do you want me to get my boys?'

The teenagers ignored him. However, the police believe that their adversary then called the group of men who attacked them. The pair was waiting at another bus stop in nearby Manchester Road when a Renault Clio screeched to a halt close by. Four men got out. Fearing for their safety, the pair fled. The men then chased them through the streets of Mossley.

Pourabolghassiam was tackled and brought to the ground by one man, who has never been traced. Wielding a knife, Hill then sat on top of him and stabbed him three times in the chest and arm while Livesley kicked him, punched him and stamped on his head. His sixteen-year-old friend was also caught nearby by other members of the gang and punched and kicked.

Delaney was in no way involved. He was simply driving by when he saw Hill and Livesley. Horrified by the brutality of their attack on Pourabolghassiam, Delaney stopped his van, jumped out and pitched in. He kicked Hill in the head with such force he broke his jaw and knocked him unconscious. Then he punched Livesley and split his nose. He later told police he believed that the pair would not have stopped their vicious attack if he had not intervened. He remained with the victim until an ambulance arrived.

Pourabolghassiam was taken to hospital where it was discovered that one of the stab wounds had penetrated his chest wall and was potentially life-threatening. He was kept in hospital under observation for several days. After his discharge, he recovered well from his injuries, but continued to suffer flashbacks of the assault.

Hill and Livesley were also taken to hospital. At the magistrate's court, Hill pleaded guilty to wounding with intent and Livesley pleaded guilty to wounding, but they went on to the Crown court to face charges of grievous bodily harm.

The court was told that Thomas Delaney saw the attack happening and got out of his vehicle to go to Mr Pourabolghassiam's aid.

The prosecutor Mark Monaghan said: 'He ran over and kicked Hill in order to bring the incident to an end. The kick from Mr Delaney knocked Hill unconscious. He then kicked Daniel Livesley, which stopped him attacking the victim. Mr Pourabolghassiam was taken to hospital. He had two defensive wounds to the upper front of his right arm. And what looks like a smaller wound on the lower side of his chest was potentially life-threatening. Hill was also taken to hospital with a fracture to his jaw.'

Defending Hill, Mark Fireman said: 'He is not a man with any violence on his record. This is clearly an act which is utterly out of character.'

Fireman maintained that Hill, himself, had taken action as a vigilante, coming to the aid of his mate.

'This incident was provoked – rightly or wrongly –

by the fact that he received a telephone call,' Fireman said. 'His understanding was that someone had been injured by the victim.'

Defending Livesley, Hunter Gray made the same point: 'He was involved in a revenge attack believing that one of his friends had been assaulted,' he said. 'He himself required eight stitches in his nose.'

Judge Goldstone did not accept Hill and Livesley's vigilante defence.

'You two were part of a posse of five who went to search out two men who you believed, quite wrongly, had assaulted your friend,' he said. 'You, Hill, sat on top of your victim and stabbed him three times, the third penetrated his chest wall. It was potentially life-threatening but mercifully it didn't penetrate his lung so there was no internal bleeding. I have no doubt that the attack would have continued had it not been for the brave and timely intervention of Thomas Delaney. I would like to commend the bravery and public spirit of Mr Delaney.'

He also said he would be writing to the Greater Manchester Police Chief Constable Peter Fahy to recommend Delaney for a commendation. Meanwhile the newspapers dubbed Delaney a modern-day Good Samaritan.

The judge jailed Hill for seven years. Livesley was given a two-year community service order and tagged. Judge Goldstone also said the injuries they sustained at the hands of Mr Delaney were 'nothing more than they deserved'.

Speaking for the Greater Manchester Police, Detective Constable Kimberley Hines said: 'This was a horrendous and violent assault. I am in no doubt that Hill and Livesley would have continued their vicious attack if the member of the public had not intervened and if that had happened I could easily have been dealing with a murder investigation. The victim was simply walking his friend to get the bus home and instead ended up seriously ill in hospital.'

That was one case where vigilante action paid off. But things don't always work out that way. Thirty-eight-year-old have-a-go hero William Carr, of Prospect Avenue, Darwen, Lancashire, was jailed after carrying out a vigilante attack on a boy he thought had attacked an elderly woman. He had come to the aid of the pensioner after she was set upon by four men on 18 July 2009. As a result he was hit on the head and left with a gaping wound.

Four days later, on Anyon Street, he saw a sixteen-year-old boy whom he believed to have been involved, and bundled him into a van. Carr was then alleged to have assaulted the boy. He menaced the boy with a trowel and threatened to cut his fingers off. The incident lasted around a minute. During that time the van had travelled around two hundred yards. The young man was then let out.

Defence barrister Richard Bennett told Preston Crown court that Carr had made a 'citizen's arrest that went too far'. Carr had suffered serious head injury from the previous incident and there was no doubt in his mind that the boy had been a part of the group responsible.

'His case has always been that he was going to take the complainant to a police station,' said Bennett. 'When matters had calmed down, he decided that what he was doing was very foolish and the young man was let out of the van. He realises he cannot take the law into his own hands and that clearly his actions were disproportionate.'

Carr pleaded guilty to a charge of false imprisonment and was jailed for nine months.

Recorder Mark Ainsworth told Carr: 'This court cannot allow people to take such matters into their own hands. This court cannot tolerate or permit vigilante justice.'

After the case, Detective Constable Mark Cruise said: 'This was an unprovoked attack on a teenage boy and I am satisfied with the sentence. Carr believed the boy was responsible for assaulting him previously but this does not compensate for the level of violence he used. I hope it serves as a warning to those who take the law into their own hands, that they will be thoroughly investigated and could face a prison sentence.'

Another vigilante who suffered for his pains was 45-year-old Paul Yarwood, who lost his job as a train guard after he tackled a boozy yob. He was hauled through the courts and charged with threatening behaviour. A drunken fare-dodger was abusing passengers and had threatened them with a broom handle on Colchester North station when Paul Yarwood, who had worked for One Railway for seven years, came to their rescue. He led passengers to safety. He then claimed he challenged the yob but was knocked to the ground, with the man looming over him. As he got up, Yarwood said, their heads collided. However, CCTV footage showed that Yarwood, a former soldier who had served for fourteen years, headbutted the man.

While the fare-dodger escaped with a fine of £80, Yarwood was summarily sacked. Hundreds of colleagues walked out in support when his union, the RMT, called two strikes over his dismissal. Yarwood was then charged with threatening behaviour and sent for trial. However, when the CCTV footage came to light, he admitted the charge and escaped with a caution.

After years of being intimidated by yobs who smashed his windows, Tory councillor Fred Brown found himself up against a young thug causing trouble in his launderette in Littleport in Cambridgeshire. The police were called, but did not turn up. Luke Rainford was kicking one of the machines, so Brown told him and his two friends to leave. They went into the optician's next door. Brown followed them in case they caused further trouble. Rainford spat at him and made headbutting gestures. Outside, the boy walked towards him waving a fist.

Fearing he was about to be hit, Brown slapped him on the side of his head to push him away. When Brown's wife stepped in, Rainford called her a 'fat cow' and spat in her face. However, when the police turned up, Brown was charged with assault. Though Brown suffered from a heart condition, arthritis and was recovering from skin cancer, he was forced to make several court appearances.

Asked in court why he had not waited for the police to arrive he said: 'Everyone in Littleport knows that if you call the police on a Monday you are likely to get them on a Wednesday.'

Eventually, he was acquitted. Hamish Ross, the chairman of the bench said: 'We find the force he used was indeed reasonable because, in the absence of police which he had requested, he felt a duty of care to staff in the optician's and to customers.'

It is estimated that the court case cost between £10,000 and £15,000.

CHAPTER 4
CITIZEN'S ARREST

When 44-year-old businessman Simon Cremer discovered his employee Mark Gilbert had forged his signature on a company cheque for £845, he bound Gilbert's hands and frogmarched him through the streets of Witham, Essex, to the police station. As a result Cremer was arrested and charged with false imprisonment – an offence that carries a maximum sentence of life.

Cremer had employed 33-year-old Gilbert at his business In House Flooring six months before, paying him up to £1,000 a week, and he was very angry because he had put a lot of trust in him. He discovered the cheque scam when he was contacted by Cash Converters, a cheque-cashing service, after the cheque bounced because it was drawn on a business account that was no longer active. Then when Gilbert came in to pick up his wages, Cremer and three other employees made a citizen's arrest.

'Four of us wrestled him to the ground,' Cremer said. 'We took his keys because he had tools in his van. When we got to the police station we handed him and the keys over.'

On the way, they marched Gilbert 350 yards down a busy shopping street with the sign around his neck, saying: 'THIEF – I stole £845, am on my way to the police station'.

'Simon didn't want to humiliate him,' said a friend of Cremer. 'He wanted other people to know.'

However, when he delivered Gilbert to the police station, he was told: 'You can't go around tying people up.'

'I don't regret what I did,' said Cremer. 'But in hind-sight it wasn't the wisest decision ... I thought I was making a citizen's arrest. Looking back I should just have called the police.'

Gilbert, a carpet-fitter at Cremer's flooring firm, was let off with a caution after admitting forging the cheque. Under a scheme designed to prevent the courts being clogged up with less serious crimes, the police have discretion to offer a caution if the person admits their guilt. Although it is not formally considered a criminal conviction, a caution is recorded on the police data-base. Whitehall statistics show tens of thousands of serious criminals – including rapists and paedophiles – receive only a caution, and the number of criminals being sent to jail is at its lowest level for a decade.

'I am not happy at all that he has been released with a caution,' said Cremer. 'I can't believe the police system. This is a guy who is a proven thief, he stole a cheque, forged a signature and took money by deception: surely there's enough to charge him there, but no, he's been let off with a caution … I'm pretty gutted, to be honest, I cannot believe that someone can do that and get away with a caution and I've been charged with false imprisonment. I'm shocked.'

Gilbert claimed that he took the money as it was owed to him in wages when Cremer was too busy to write out a cheque. He threatened to sue for humiliation and upset over the incident and told a harrowing tale about his 'arrest' when he was called into the office to pick up his wages.

'We had a bit of idle chit-chat and I turned my back and I was set upon,' he said. 'They laid into me, they beat me, I was begging Simon to let me go to the police, they said they didn't trust me and they had to tie me up. They were punching me and threatened me with various tools. They showed me the sign and made me say it out loud three times.'

Then they put him in the back of a van and he feared that they were going to kill him.

'I was tied up, I was face down and I kept trying to twist round,' he said. 'They stopped at the pub, so they could march me through the streets. I wished the world would swallow me up, I hoped no one would recognise me. It was almost a relief when I saw the police station was in sight rather than a remote field.'

Gilbert, from Colchester in Essex, admitted making a business cheque out to himself and taking it to the cheque-cashing service Cash Converters. He claimed the money was what he was due as his weekly payment, and his boss was too busy to write it. However, he was too frightened to go through with the fraud. He paid the money back to Cash Converters, he said, and believed the matter was finished. But Cash Converters contacted Cremer, prompting his furious reaction.

Gilbert was taken to Braintree police station where he was questioned and released at 3 a.m. after being cautioned. Cremer and the employees who had made the 'arrest' were held overnight. Officers told Gilbert on his release: 'You've got a bigger case against them.'

Even Gilbert was shocked. 'I'm the criminal here,' he said. He also said he was pleased he had been let off with a caution but did not want his former boss and colleagues to go to prison.

'I feel for them and I don't want anything bad to happen to them,' he said. 'But it wasn't really correct what they did to me.'

Gilbert claims he suffered bruises to his body and side, a black eye, an injured hip and marks on his wrists from the ropes. He said of Mr Cremer: 'I feel for the bloke, I respect the bloke, but I want him to pay for what he's done.'

Cremer was fingerprinted, forced to give a DNA sample, which will remain on record, and kept in the cells overnight. The newspapers then picked up on the story and he became an instant celebrity.

'Ten days ago, if you'd tapped my name into the internet, one entry would have come up saying "carpet fitter",' he said after his arrest. 'By yesterday, my name had been mentioned 275,000 times. I never expected this. I don't want to be famous. I just wish it would all go away.'

Cremer was released at eleven the following morning, returning home to his partner of six years, doctor's receptionist Karen Boardman, 44, who was frantic with worry. Seeing Karen – who was battling breast cancer – so upset was, he said, the worst part of all.

'When I saw her in tears, I felt terrible,' he said. 'She would have had every right to be angry with me because she had no idea what I was planning. It wasn't until I was lying in the police cell, unable to sleep with worry, that I realised I was in serious trouble and might even go to prison. Karen's been through enough this past year with her health and doesn't need the stress, but if I'd thought for one second I'd end up getting arrested I would never have done it. I had no idea I was breaking the law.'

Cremer also contested Gilbert's version of the events.

'He wasn't face down,' said Cremer. 'He was sitting up. We'd put carpet down so he wouldn't get hurt when we put him in the back.'

However, he admitted that they stopped in the car park of the White Hart pub, where they took Gilbert out of the van, put the placard around his neck and marched him down the High Street.

To many, Cremer, a hard-working father of two, was a modern-day hero. Some newspapers portrayed him as a man prepared to hand out summary justice in an age when the rights of the accused were placed above those of the victim. He was a hard-pressed family man driven to the end of his tether by the financial crisis engulfing so many. But others accused Cremer of taking the law into his own hands and indulging in a lynch-mob mentality. His vigilante action was seen as a disturbing throwback to medieval times when the accused were humiliated in the pillory without the charges against them having been proved in court.

'I genuinely thought I was making a citizen's arrest,' said Cremer. 'I wouldn't have marched him down the street and taken him to the police station if I thought I was doing anything wrong. I'm a small businessman, struggling to survive the credit crunch, sometimes working twenty-hour days to make a living, and I need to be able to trust the subcontractors I employ. My reputation is built on honesty and I felt I'd been betrayed, which hurt me.'

Despite the charges against him, Cremer felt entirely justified in his action.

'I would never have done this if £845 hadn't been taken from my firm without my knowledge,' he said. 'I have never spent a night in a police cell before in my life. I'm a law-abiding citizen. I thought I was standing up for all the honest, decent people of this community. Never in a million years did I imagine it would end up like this.'

The consequences he faced were dire for all concerned.

'If I'm convicted, I'll probably lose my business and several people will be out of work,' he acknowledged. 'Yes, I should have just called the police in the first place. But let's face it: this kind of allegation – though important to me – comes pretty low down on their list of priorities. I was worried that they'd take half an hour to turn up and by that time Mark could have just disappeared. I was determined to take him to them, because I wanted the community to know exactly what I was accusing him of. I confiscated his car keys so he couldn't just drive away and handed those over to the police, too.'

His arrest came as a complete shock.

'I was stunned, completely shell-shocked, when I was

arrested as well,' he said. 'I'm not angry with the police, but surely their time would be better spent locking up real criminals. I'm not a danger to anyone.'

His partner Karen was totally supportive, although she accepts that what he did may have been wrong in the eyes of the law.

'When Simon told me what had happened, I know I should have been cross, but when he explained his reasons, I couldn't be angry with him,' she said. 'It's not the way I would have chosen to handle the situation, but Simon did it for the right reasons. He would hardly have walked into a police station if he'd thought he'd done anything wrong. Simon is an ordinary, decent, hard-working person. He's not a vigilante.'

However, she admitted knowing that Cremer intended to confront Gilbert over the cheque.

'When he told me about the cheque that had been cashed and that he was going to confront Mark about it, I said, "Be careful." I was more worried about Simon getting hurt because Mark is a big guy and you don't know how people will react in these situations.'

Nevertheless, how things panned out came as a surprise.

'The first I knew of the walk of shame was when Simon's daughter Natalie phoned me and said: "Dad's walking down the street with Mark, who's got a placard round his neck. What's going on?" I couldn't tell her because I didn't have a clue.'

Things then went from bad to worse.

'When Simon phoned me from the police station to tell me he was in trouble with the police, I was stunned, but neither of us knew just how bad it might be. That night I kept looking at the clock and thinking: "Why isn't Simon home yet?" When he came home the following day he was wearing a blue sweatshirt, jogging bottoms and plimsolls. I asked, "Where are your clothes?" They'd taken the clothes he was wearing and given him a brand new set. I thought: "So that's where taxpayers' money is going." Instead of being used to catch real criminals, it's being spent on jogging suits and plimsolls for people like Simon. I still can't understand why the police felt they needed to put him in a cell for the night. Simon isn't a dangerous criminal.'

According to Karen there was support in the community for what Cremer had done.

'I work in a doctor's surgery and people who have no idea I'm associated with Simon have come in with their newspaper and said: "Good for him." What Simon did was wrong, but I think a lot of people would secretly love to do the same thing, given the chance.'

Karen, too, was outraged when Gilbert got off with a caution. 'I am disgusted,' she said. 'I have no faith left in the British justice system. The person that committed the crime has walked away, completely free. He will be sitting at home over Christmas, without a care, while Simon and the other three, who are all family men, have this hanging over them. Their judgement was maybe clouded slightly because times are tough and this man had taken money from the business which provides their livelihoods. But I will not condemn what they've done. Even giving them a caution would be wrong.'

Karen had a mastectomy the previous March. She had just completed a course of chemotherapy and was due to have her other breast removed the following January.

'We've had a difficult year and just don't need this added stress,' she said. 'Simon has taken a lot of time off work to care for me while I've had breast cancer. He took his eye off the ball at work and I believe someone took advantage of that. And now Simon is going to pay for it.'

To make up his earnings lost during the legal proceedings, Cremer had to work day and night without a break. As the boss of In House Flooring of Witham, which he set up eight years before, he pays himself between £2,000 and £2,500 a month – less than Gilbert and the other sub-contractors he employs. On that he had to support Karen during her illness and two teenage daughters from a previous marriage.

'I could make more money as a fitter,' said Cremer. 'But I am trying to build up a successful business of my own, which is hard in today's economic climate.'

Cremer hired Gilbert – a father of three – after he had been laid off by another company. He said he offered Gilbert a job because he felt sorry for him and wanted to give him a chance. However, Gilbert did not live up to expectations.

'The quality of his work really wasn't up to scratch,' said Cremer. 'But every time I spoke to Mark about it he'd promise to do a better job next time, saying, "I won't let you down." So I would keep on giving him another chance, only to be let down time and time again. He wouldn't turn up for jobs, sending me text messages explaining that he was dealing with some family tragedy or another. I have no idea if these were true or not, but I'm the kind of person who likes to give someone the benefit of the doubt.'

But things only came to a head when Cremer received the call from Cash Converters.

'Mark claims the money was what he was due and that I was too busy to write the cheque,' said Cremer, 'but I paid him every week on time. If it wasn't the Friday, then it would be the Monday.'

Even then he wanted to give Gilbert a chance to explain himself.

'When Cash Converters sent me a photocopy of the cheque, I should have called the police then, but I wanted to sit Mark down, look him in the eye and ask him to explain because I felt he'd betrayed my trust completely.'

But he was taking no chances.

'I'd told a few colleagues what I planned to do and they agreed to help,' said Cremer. 'What I was worried about most is what might happen when I confronted Mark. I didn't want it to turn into a fist fight, with someone ending up getting hurt. I haven't been in a fight since I was in school, but I didn't know how Mark might react. There are a lot of dangerous tools around the offices, so I decided it would be safer for everyone if we restrained him.'

Cremer was adamant that that was as far as it went.

'We didn't beat him up or threaten him with tools, but we did wrestle him to the ground,' he said. 'If he got bruised as he was flailing around, then I'm sorry for that, but no punches were thrown. None of it was done out of temper or for revenge. We sat him on a chair and I showed him the cheque. He kept saying how sorry he was and begged me not to call the police. From the start, I told him very calmly what would happen. I told him that we weren't going to hurt him. The whole thing lasted only fifteen minutes.'

Throughout Gilbert insisted that he had written the cheque out to himself because it was what he believed he was due.

'I was leaving the country to start a new life in Cyprus,' he said. 'I couldn't raise my cheque, so I thought I'd write one out myself. He was too busy and I was in a rush to go. It was for my week's wages. I even took off the 20 per cent tax. I could have taken £10,000, but I took only what I believed was due to me. We all do stupid things.'

Cremer said he had several phone messages from Gilbert after the event where Gilbert invited him to meet in a public place, so they could sort the problem out amicably. However, Cremer was not interested in talking to Gilbert given the legal wrangle he found himself in. He said his biggest regret is hiring Gilbert in the first place.

Cremer received numerous messages of support from friends and strangers alike. Many share his frustration that criminals get nothing more than a slap on the wrist from our overstretched justice system while law-abiding citizens take the rap. One stranger even offered to pay any fine Cremer might incur if he was convicted.

'I know now what I did was wrong, but at no stage did I think I was breaking the law,' said Cremer. 'I'm not looking for sympathy. I did what I did, it was wrong and I'll just have to accept the consequences ... I don't regret my action, the fact I tied his hands is the only bit I regret.'

However, on 20 December 2008, Simon Cremer and the three other men who had helped him arrest Gilbert – his brother, Andrew, 42, David White, 42, and Reece Bennett, 23 – walked free from court after the case against them was dismissed when they agreed to be bound over to keep the peace for year.

'At the end of the day, nothing's come of it, so it does seem like a lot of rigmarole, to be honest,' he said after the case was closed. 'We are pleased at the treatment we've had today but I'm not convinced a caution was the right action for Mr Gilbert.'

The use of the citizen's right to make an arrest has got other people into trouble with the law. One of them was 45-year-old construction worker Stuart Hicks, of Albion Terrace, Whitby. He had a running battle with neighbour Duncan Grimshaw who, Hicks said, had subjected the neighbourhood to a prolonged campaign of vandalism, theft and abuse. Hicks said that his car had vandalised by Grimshaw. His family was subjected repeatedly to foul and abusive language by Grimshaw who also threatened to burn their house down. The threats also extended to Hicks's son Shane, who was deeply affected.

'One day he threatened to pour petrol over my nine-year-old son, who is still traumatised and always locks the door,' said Hicks. 'I always went to the police and they told me not to take things into my own hands and not to be a vigilante.'

It was advice he would not take.

On 13 June 2007 Hicks had noticed Grimshaw, who had already been banned from entering Albion Terrace, acting suspiciously next to his car, which had been vandalised the day before. There was a confrontation and Hicks tried to make a citizen's arrest.

'I rugby-tackled him to the floor and he was trying to bite my knee and my leg,' said Hicks. 'I may have inadvertently kneed him in the face but I pinned him down and rang the police.'

When officers arrived they arrested Hicks, who spent nine hours in a cell. At Scarborough magistrates' court he pleaded not guilty to a public order offence. Meanwhile, York Crown court substantiated Hicks's allegations. In August 2007 26-year-old Grimshaw, of Green Lane Campsite, Whitby, was jailed for three years and seventy-six days after admitting sixty-four offences, mainly relating to burglary, theft and dishonesty.

At a further hearing the charge against Hicks was dismissed when he agreed to be bound over in the sum of £100 to keep the peace for six months. However, he still resents being taken to court.

'For me to make a citizen's arrest and then have to go through all this is disgusting,' he said. 'The way I have been treated is disgraceful.'

However, Hicks was pleased Grimshaw had been taken off the streets but said he should have been locked up for longer.

'My son was crying all the time, asking if this man was going to pour petrol over him,' said Hicks. 'Eventually, I made a citizen's arrest because I believed that

I was doing the right thing. I would do exactly the same thing again because I don't believe I did anything wrong.'

CHAPTER 5
VIGILANTES VINDICATED

Workers at a city minicab firm were accused of putting out a coded SOS call to orchestrate a vigilante attack on three troublesome passengers. Peterborough Crown court was told that staff in the cab firm's control room in the Millfield area of the city issued a 'Code 786' – an emergency call summoning all drivers in the area to mete out their own brand of justice to the trouble-makers. However, when the passengers were dropped off at Peterborough Cars' base, it was three taxi workers who ended up hospitalised after apparently being punched, kicked and beaten with a steel wheel-brace.

The passengers – 33-year-old Hitpreet Virdee, Lee White and Samuel Needham, both 27 – were jointly accused of assaulting the cab men and causing griev-ous bodily harm after a fare dispute spiralled out of control. They denied all charges against them, claim-ing that it was the cab company's staff who initiated the violence.

One of the injured men, control room worker Nahim

Hanif, told the court how he was attacked by two of the three defendants after they arrived outside his office in Rock Road, Millfield, and maintained that the violence had not been initiated by him and his colleagues.

Prosecutor Hugh Vass asked: 'Are you familiar with a Code 786?'

'Yes, it means emergency, driver needs help,' Hanif replied. 'If he was being attacked or if he was in trouble, he would use that code. But it is not used frequently, and I don't believed it was used that night.'

The incident took place in the early hours of Sunday, 27 July 2008 after minicab driver Waheed Iqbal picked up the three men. Then, after a dispute over the fare, he drove them to the headquarters of Peterborough Cars. An altercation ensued and Hanif was left needing stitches in a number of deep cuts on his head after being hit repeatedly with a wheel-brace. Iqbal and colleague Mohammed Mushtaq were also badly injured.

Under cross-examination, Hanif was asked if he was injured only after he and his colleagues had wielded weapons and attacked the three defendants.

But he angrily denied the suggestion, adding: 'If you look at the photographs [of the injuries], you will realise which are the people who were hurt and which are the people who weren't.'

Speaking with the help of an interpreter, Iqbal claimed he had been verbally abused and punched by Virdee, so he drove to his base. Then, when the violent confrontation continued after the men had got out of the car, he had foolishly grabbed a wheel-brace from his boot to protect himself.

'When they saw me with the wheel-brace in my hand, the white men [White and Needham] ran towards me,' he said. 'The Indian man [Virdee] got into my car and drove it with great force towards me. He was going to run me over, but I jumped out of the way. As I moved, my face turned towards the white men and one of them punched me in the face. I fell down and after that they started beating me up.'

He was punched and kicked unconscious, waking up to find himself in hospital, but not before seeing Virdee grab the wheel-brace and attack Peterborough Cars controllers Mohammed Mushtaq and Nahim Hanif, hitting Mushtaq repeatedly around the head. The attack left him on the brink of unconsciousness and with head injuries so severe that he has since been told by doctors he can never drive a taxi for a living again.

The three defendants deny assault and causing grievous bodily harm, claiming they were kidnapped by Iqbal and driven to his base where they were attacked by a gang of vigilante cabbies waiting with weapons to ambush them. Any injuries caused to the victims, they said, happened as they struggled to escape the scene.

Eyewitness Leonard Donnelly contradicted this. He said he had watched in horror from his bedroom window as a taxi driver and two of his colleagues were viciously assaulted in the street by the three men, who then ran away laughing.

'There was a taxi in the middle of the street with its door open and I saw two taxi drivers who I recognised arguing with three other men,' Donnelly said. 'I wasn't sure what was going to happen until I saw what looked like a metal cosh being produced by one of the three men. It was an extendable metal cosh because he flicked it out and it extended. I saw him strike one of the taxi drivers around the head. It was kind of a base-ball swing.'

Donnelly said that the attack continued when one of the three defendants got into the driver's seat of the taxi and drove a short distance down the street. The three men then fled the scene.

Prosecutor Hugh Vass asked Mr Donnelly: 'Were you able to hear anything as they ran off?'

'Just laughter, generally,' said Donnelly. 'Laughter coming from them.'

In their defence, the accused claimed they had been led into a trap by the driver who had picked them up. Virdee said Waheed Iqbal drove them to the head-quarters of Peterborough Cars to be greeted by several of his colleagues armed with metal bars. He told jurors he had acted only in self-defence as he tried to flee the scene in desperation.

The three men were returning to the city from a wedding at the Haycock Hotel, in Wansford, Virdee said, when their driver veered away from the direct route.

'We'd asked how much the fare was going to be,' he said. 'He told us ten pounds, but then changed it to fifteen pounds on the way. I was having a laugh and a joke and said the three of us would pay a pound each. It was a bit of banter, but obviously he took it the wrong way.'

Virdee told the court the driver began talking on his mobile phone and was 'effing and blinding', before driving them straight to his headquarters in Rock Road, Millfield.

'Once the car stopped the taxi driver got out and pulled a metal cosh out of the driver's side door. Sam opened the door and we all followed him out,' Virdee said. 'There were six or seven people waiting there and he came towards us with this cosh. I was angry because we had wanted to go to the city centre but we ended up at a taxi rank with guys who were armed with metal bars.'

Virdee told the court he pushed two of the victims as he tried to run away, but did not hit any of them.

'I just wanted to get out of there,' he said. 'I wasn't in a position to have a fight with anyone because I've been hit with a metal bar before and ended up in hospital with serious injuries. If someone had done it again I would probably be six feet under.'

After a six-day trial, the jury took four and a half hours to decide unanimously that Hitpreet Virdee was responsible for causing grievous bodily harm to Mohammed Mushtaq. His two co-defendants, Lee White and Samuel Needham, were cleared of any involvement in the attack. Virdee was also found guilty of affray after being captured on CCTV in a scuffle outside a city-centre bar later the same evening, and has admitted a further charge of affray relating to a separate incident a few weeks before the attack. As a result the vigilante cab drivers were vindicated.

CHAPTER 6
NAME AND SHAME

The *News of the World*'s 'name-and-shame' anti-paedophile campaign following the abduction and murder of eight-year-old Sarah Payne in 2000 was blamed for sparking vigilante action. On 23 July 2000, the newspaper printed the names and photographs of forty-nine people and gave the town or district where they lived. It vowed to identify all 110,000 child sex offenders living in the UK, saying the move was aimed at alerting and warning the public about those named and was 'not a charter for vigilantes'. However, the paper's action led to angry mobs terrorising those they suspected of being child sex offenders.

An innocent man who was mistaken for one of the paedophiles named and shamed had his home attacked. Forty-nine-year-old Iain Armstrong from the Beswick area of Greater Manchester was confronted by locals in the street after vigilantes thought he was one of the child abusers named in the *News of the World*.

As he suffers from a spinal disorder, Armstrong was wearing a neck-brace similar to one worn by a paedophile pictured in the paper. After being confronted in the street, he had a panic button installed in his house. It was activated at nine o'clock that night when a brick was thrown through the window of his former wife's home next door. Armstrong had been watching television with two of his sons when he heard people from neighbouring streets chanting 'paedophile' outside. After alerting the police, he went outside to show them his passport and driving licence to prove they had got the wrong man. The police arrived to find twelve women and children outside his house.

'They were saying, "Here he is, here he comes",' Armstrong said, 'and the policeman was saying it's not who you think it is.'

Not only was Armstrong entirely innocent of the allegation of being a sex offender, he told the crowd he had the same fear of paedophiles as readers of the *News of the World*.

'So I looked at them and said, "I have got three kids of my own. I don't want one of them living near me same as you don't",' he said.

The crowd moved off after being spoken to by the officers. No one was arrested for the damage.

Assistant Chief Constable Alan Green said the attack was an 'irresponsible reaction to emotive stories in a national newspaper' and he warned people against taking vigilante action.

'Greater Manchester Police will take the strongest possible action against those who take the law into their own hands,' he said. 'This incident demonstrates how people with no connections to these stories can become victims.'

Other police chiefs, probation officers and other experts also criticised the *News of the World*'s name-and-shame campaign. Home Office minister Paul Boateng said the newspaper's action was 'unhelpful' and Shadow Home Secretary Ann Widdecombe said: 'This incident shows that the *News of the World*, whatever their intentions may have been, are inciting a lynch-mob mentality.'

Editor of the *News of the World* Rebekah Wade was unrepentant. Although the newspaper did not condone vigilante attacks, she said, 'every parent has an absolute right to know if they have a convicted child offender living in their neighbourhood. The disturbing truth is that the authorities are failing to properly monitor the activities of paedophiles in the community. The continued support of Sarah's family for our campaign plus the overwhelming public support means that the *News of the World* will continue its long tradition of exposing and investigating those who are a danger to our society.'

As a result of the campaign, the police also had to give protection to 55-year-old Michael Horgan after 500 leaflets wrongly accusing him of being a child abuser were distributed by a vigilante group calling itself Anti-matter to houses near his home in south London. Horgan said: 'The police are treating it very seriously. At first I thought it was a hoax. My mother brought a letter in – she was in a state of shock.'

The police then had the job of tracing the sources of the leaflets.

'This malicious letter has caused Mr Horgan and his family considerable distress,' said Detective Inspector Steve Lamb of Lewisham CID. 'It has taken up an enormous amount of police time in countering the allegation, and at considerable expense to the taxpayer.'

The police also had to give protection to a man in the Guildford area after he was wrongly identified as a convicted paedophile in a series of malicious letters.

The situation then escalated. Over five days in August, hundreds of people took to the streets in the Paulsgrove district of Portsmouth. The protest began peacefully but ended with demonstrators throwing stones and other missiles. Windows were broken. The property of a man whose name was not on the sex-offender's register was ransacked. Police were forced to don protective headgear when stones, coins and eggs were thrown at them. A police sergeant was hospitalised and a car belonging to a resident overturned and set on fire, forcing police to evacuate residents under threat.

One man was arrested for assaulting a police officer. Thirteen others were detained in disturbances outside alleged paedophiles' homes in two areas of the estate. Deputy Chief Constable of Hampshire Police Ian Reedhead warned violent protests would not help the situation.

'We can have an informed and intellectual debate,' he said, 'but you can't do that at the end of a house brick. It is one thing to talk about access to information. But once you make it general in nature then unfortunately it won't be the mums and dads who are concerned about their children's safety who have access. It will be a much wider community, some of whom are prepared to take vigilante action.'

The riots prompted Portsmouth MP Sydney Rapson to call for suspected child abusers in the area to be moved out. He also said that outsiders were flocking to the area to cause trouble for trouble's sake.

'The police are doing their job, protecting life and property, and in doing that, it is seen by the crowd as protecting the suspect,' said the MP.

Rapson and councillors for the area affected met the acting leader of Portsmouth city council to ask for alleged paedophiles to be moved from the estate.

'If all these people can be moved out, that will take away the point of contention,' Rapson said. Four families with no connection to paedophiles also asked to be rehoused following the riots.

By this time, Rebekah Wade had already backed down and the newspaper had announced that it was halting the publication of names following protests from the government, police and care authorities, who were worried it would drive paedophiles underground. Nevertheless, vigilante attacks continued on the guilty and innocent alike.

The home of 56-year-old Roger Gardener in Blackwood, Gwent, was damaged by fire while he was awaiting sentencing for assaulting two girls aged twelve and thirteen over a five-year period. Police officers had to accompany fire crews who were called to tackle the fire at 11 p.m. on 17 August. The police said they were treating the fire as suspicious.

Gardener, an unemployed lorry driver, had been found guilty at Cardiff Crown court of indecently assaulting two young cadets from a St John Ambulance group run by his wife, 52-year-old auxiliary nurse Margaret. She stuck up for him, protesting his innocence from the public gallery, but the judge, William Gaskell, reassured the jury that they were 'wholly justified' in their guilty verdict. The vigilantes agreed. It was while the case was adjourned for pre-sentence reports and Gardener released on bail that the arsonist struck.

The family of a convicted paedophile in Flintshire, North Wales, was hounded by local people after the husband was jailed. They were victimised, it was said, following the publicity surrounding the name-and-shame campaign. After one incident, the man's daughter fled in her pyjamas, jumped into her red pickup truck and drove off – only to crash into an oncoming BMW car, causing £2,600-worth of damage. She then gave a false name and fled the scene. However, she returned later to give her true name to the police. In court she admitted failing to stop after an accident, driving without a licence, having no insurance and no MOT, and was put on probation for a year.

The most notorious vigilante attack after the name-and-shame campaign was on the home of South African-born Yvette Cloete – a 30-year-old trainee consultant paediatrician at the Royal Gwent Hospital, Newport, South Wales – who returned home on 24 August 2000 to find the word 'paedo' daubed across the front of her house. It was thought that vigilantes had mistaken her job title – paediatrician – for the word paedophile.

'I'm really a victim of ignorance,' she said. 'It is just unbelievable. It is terrible that people think that they have the right to vandalise your property like this no matter what you have done. We telephoned the police immediately and began to clean off the words as soon as we could. You think that your home is a place to go to be safe so it is a shock when something like this happens.'

She went to stay with friends and vowed never to return to the house, which she rented.

CHAPTER 7
PAEDOPHILE ATTACKS

Paedophiles have long been the target of vigilante attacks. In 1997, Scottish crime queen Mags Haney led a gang of vigilantes who hounded a notorious paedophile out of the Raploch estate in Stirling which she and her clan used to terrorise. She even went on the *Kilroy* TV show, claiming to speak for local people. But months later, Haney became the victim of vigilante action herself when she and her family were driven from their home by 400 neighbours who were fed up with their antics. In 2000, she was exposed by the *Daily Record* as the leader of a £1,000-a-day heroin empire and finally jailed for twelve years for drug offences in 2003. Her daughter Diane, 35, was sentenced to nine years, niece Roseann, 40, to seven years and son Hugh, 31, to five years at the High Court in Edinburgh. The vigilante grandmother had previous convictions stretching back to 1975 for offences including assault, breach of the peace, fraud and contempt of court.

Fear of attack by vigilantes led a registered sex offender to go on the run abroad after being freed from prison. Joseph Millbank, 48, of Luncarty, Perthshire, who was jailed in 2002 for sex attacks on thirty-two little girls aged three to eight, was caught in sun-drenched St Tropez on the French Riviera after an international manhunt. He said he fled because the police told him they would have to tell neighbours of his whereabouts after his release and he felt he would be at risk of possible violence. He pleaded guilty to breaching Sex Offenders' Register rules. Those on the register must notify the police if they are intending to travel abroad.

The elderly mother of a paedophile in Bedworth, near Coventry, was physically attacked by vigilantes who had read about the case in the press. As a result, she suffered a stroke. Wayne John Haywood, who sexually abused a thirteen-year-old girl while celebrating his fortieth birthday, gave himself up to the police a few days later. He was jailed for eighteen months and placed on the Sex Offenders' Register for ten years.

Another alleged paedophile was killed fleeing a baying mob of vigilantes threatening to murder him, Manchester Crown court was told. Glaswegian Scott Campbell, aged 44, fell fifty feet from the balcony of his second-floor flat in Deane, Bolton, when the gang, armed with a baseball bat, a hammer, a wrench and a bike chain, stormed the block after he was accused of a sex attack on a boy of thirteen. The boy had gone to Campbell's flat to buy marijuana, when Campbell tried to yank his trousers down. Campbell was a convicted sex offender. He was jailed for a total of six years in 1995 – including five years for committing a sexual assault. After his death, detectives found a mobile phone in his flat containing images of young boys being sexually abused.

'My friend told us he was going to the guy's for some weed,' his thirteen-year-old mate told Manchester Crown court. 'After about fifteen to twenty minutes he still wasn't back. He was taking so long, I said this doesn't feel right. He came out and said, "That guy has just tried to feel me up." He had a shocked look on his face. He said he was sat in a chair and the guy pulled his trousers down.'

The story spread quickly around the area and locals gathered around the block of flats.

The defendants Jamie Watson and his wife Sarah, both 32, were seen entering the flats with 36-year-old Katia Briercliffe. They were joined in the lift by 36-year-old Paul McCarthy and 37-year-old Martin McMulkin, who lived in the block. The prosecution cited CCTV footage that purported to show Sarah Watson hiding a baseball bat up the back of her coat, Jamie Watson carrying a hammer, Briercliffe with a spanner or wrench and McMulkin holding a bicycle chain. All except McMulkin attempted to hide their faces, it was alleged.

The boy was seen on the CCTV footage pointing out the flat he had been in, before leaving. Then one of the gang banged on the front door, shouting, 'I'm going to fucking kill you.'

Campbell opened his door but quickly slammed it when he realised what was happening. Prosecutor Peter Cadwallader told Manchester Crown court: 'Once he had closed the door there was an attack on it with weapons. It was struck. The glass was broken. There was banging and noise and it was so great that it was heard by neighbours. The Crown says the defendants were trying to force the door. They were a large group. They were armed. They were damaging the door and attacking it.'

In a bid to escape, Campbell climbed over his balcony, but he lost his grip on the rail and plunged to the ground while one of the baying mob screamed they would kill him and another shouted, 'You are a pervert.' He suffered multiple injuries and was pronounced dead at the Royal Bolton Hospital in Lancashire. Jamie and Sarah Watson, Katia Briercliffe, Paul McCarthy and Martin McMulkin were all arrested and held on remand for six months until the case came to trial.

Mr Cadwallader told the jury: 'Although you may have little sympathy for Mr Campbell it must have been a frightening experience and he must have been fearful of what was going to happen if they gained entry.

Whatever your sympathies are, the defendants, we say, were all acting unlawfully in trying to take the law into their own hands and act as a vigilante group. It is apparent from CCTV footage that the deceased felt under attack and went on to the balcony with the intention to lower himself down. It is equally clear that he lost his grip in trying to climb down and he fell and died as a result of injuries he sustained in the fall. The inference is that Scott Campbell was in fear as a result of the defendants' attempt to break into his flat. He must have known that he faced a beating at least. There was no other way out of the flat and it is our case that in trying to escape the unlawful conduct of the defendants he fell to his death.'

It was only after Sarah Watson had left the flats that she called the police to complain about Campbell's conduct, the prosecution alleged. Unaware that he had died, she continued to make threats about him to the police operator, saying: 'If you don't come down here, I'm going to knife him.'

Cadwallader said. 'However justified their position, it cannot be acceptable for a vigilante group to start taking the law into their own hands and that is the simple issue in this case because that is what happened. Attempts were made by the individuals to cover and hide their features, which the Crown says was indicative of what they intended.'

All the defendants denied manslaughter. Cadwallader

conceded that the sympathies of the jury might lie with the vigilantes, which seems to have been the case. Katia Briercliffe protested that she was entirely innocent. She told police she had only accompanied Sarah Watson to the block of flats because she feared she would do something 'daft'.

In court, Briercliffe said: 'I went to make sure Sarah was OK. She was upset and angry.'

But she claimed that when she said 'daft', she had meant 'shouting and screaming' – nothing more sinister. 'I thought she was just going to go upstairs and make sure that it was the right flat and phone the police,' she said, so she visited friends, her co-accused Martin McMulkin and Paul McCarthy, in a flat in the same block.

Sarah Watson told the court: 'I wanted him to know that I knew he was a paedophile. I wanted to know where he was so I could call the police.'

She denied trying to 'rush' the victim's flat so the gang could attack him. She said she wanted justice and added: 'I had no intentions of hurting that man in any way, shape or form.'

Paul McCarthy, who had only recently moved into the block of flats, told the police that he had joined the group 'to watch a slanging match'. He said that the Watsons started banging on the door with a baseball bat and a hammer, smashing the glass above the door. He added he did not think there was going to be a violent confrontation, but conceded that Campbell must have been scared.

'Never in a million years did I think it would end up like this,' he said, after learning that Campbell was dead. 'As soon as they started smashing the door, that was it – I was off. I know what you're thinking, that we've gone up as a lynch mob, but we haven't. I don't care what their problem is, all I know is I don't want to lose my flat. I wish I could turn back time.'

The jury took less than three hours to find the five defendants not guilty. Walking free from Manchester Crown court, Sarah Watson said: 'I just want to go home now and see my kids.'

Katia Briercliffe expressed remorse. 'It wasn't supposed to end how it ended,' she said. 'We only went to confront the man. We'd been locked up for something we weren't guilty of. I'm going to go home with my son and get on with the rest of my life.'

No one has been brought to court over the murder of 73-year-old convicted paedophile Gordon Boon who was found strangled in October 2008. Police suspect that he was killed by a vigilante in a revenge attack after serving a six-year jail sentence for indecent assaults on a girl of eight and two others aged thirteen. The former cider factory worker had been released on licence. His body was found dumped on wasteland at Great Witchingham, near Norwich, by walkers on

6 October. It was discovered partly covered by old fencing panels in a fly-tipping spot, yards from the Norfolk headquarters of turkey tycoon Bernard Matthews. Boon, who lived in Norwich, had blood around his nose and mouth, and one of his shoes and a sock was missing. A post-mortem found he had died from strangulation.

At his trial, it was revealed that Boon, then a married man and father of four, plied one girl with alcohol and played strip poker with her. He then took photos of her naked, and sexually abused her. Boon admitted indecent assault and two serious sex offences against the youngster, two assaults on the second girl and one on the third. However, Judge Paul Downes told Boon that he had 'failed to accept' responsibility for his actions. After he was jailed, he was placed on the Sex Offenders' Register for life and ordered to serve an extended licence of five years on his release. However, some thought he had got off lightly.

The day after Boon went missing, his son alerted police, saying his father failed to meet him for a drink as arranged. Suspecting revenge may have been a motive, the police interviewed Boon's victims in case they could shed light on the case. Detectives said they believed that the killer escaped prosecution as they thought some witnesses were refusing to come forward due to a lack of sympathy for the victim. Not everyone was unsympathetic though. A former neighbour in Boon's hometown of Attleborough, Norfolk, said: 'He was friendly, drank at the local pub and raised funds for old people's homes.'

But the police bent themselves to their task.

'We cannot live in a vigilante society,' said Detective Chief Inspector Steve Strong of Norfolk Police. 'A killer whose motive remains unclear is out there so there must be serious concerns for the public.'

A man aged 42 was later arrested on suspicion of murder. But he was released on police bail.

The police also found themselves up against a wall of silence when they were investigating a vigilante attack on the Doncaster home of sex offender Craig Markey. A fire was deliberately started after a court case involving the 27-year-old was published. Markey had been given a community sentence for keeping more than 1,100 indecent images of children on his computer.

Neighbours said that a gang of six men armed with baseball bats smashed their way into the house and looted it before starting fires in different parts of the building. After the fire Markey was rehoused by Doncaster Council at a secret location for his own safety. However, he continued to be ostracised by his colleagues at his place of work in Doncaster.

Fifty-three-year-old Anne Fleming found her house under attack by vigilantes after she admitted molesting a young girl for five years, starting when the child was just seven. Fleming, from Bellshill, north Lanarkshire, had been a trusted friend of her victim's family for more than thirty years.

The abused youngster went on to attempt suicide when she was seventeen. She then went into counselling, where the truth came out. But the teenager did not call the police at the time, fearing reliving the events during an investigation and court case would make her life even worse. Eventually, at the age of 24, the victim finally confided in an aunt and found the courage to phone Fleming and confront her about the abuse. Fleming apologised for preying on her, unaware the call was being recorded.

The court was told that Fleming has had to be moved twice for her own safety after vigilante attacks against her since she admitted molesting the victim at her home and other locations from 1991 to 1996. She was first moved to a nearby safe house when vigilantes vandalised her council house, then when word got out she had to be moved again.

'I can't condone their actions but I can also understand why people felt like that,' said her victim. 'I had been told people were angry and disgusted when they discovered the truth. She was used as a babysitter for a lot of families and they are all angry.'

Defence counsel Stephen Hughes said: 'Since this matter has come to light she has been forced to move house twice and had her windows smashed in. She continues to be the subject of harassment.'

Strathclyde Police were called to her original home four times after it was sprayed with graffiti and garden ornaments were smashed. More recently the windows of her two-bedroom council house had been boarded up with steel shutters.

'People realised who she was and were really angry,' a local said. 'She was put in a house a minute's walk from two schools. Fleming is a marked woman, people know about her sordid past.'

This is not uncommon. Some offenders have been repeatedly driven out of the areas where they tried to settle by vigilantes. In one instance the home of a sex offender was burned down, leaving the children in the family – who had been his victims – homeless as well.

Former Soviet spy Geoffrey Prime was given a new identity to protect him from vigilante attacks when he was released on licence in 2001. But it was not because of his twenty-year career in espionage during the Cold War. He was only unmasked because he was a member of a paedophile ring and then arrested for indecent assaults on girls as young as eleven. While he was in custody, his second wife, Rhona, discovered his one-time code pads in his wallet and alerted police. In 1982 Prime was sentenced to thirty-five years for spying and a further three years for three indecent assaults.

*

Public outrage at such offenders is understandable. In 2008, 25-year-old joiner Stuart McGurk, of Galashiels, Selkirkshire, was fined £200 for shouting and swearing at Andrew Finn, who had admitted in court to having pornographic pictures on his computer.

CHAPTER 8
MURDER OF THE ANIMAL

Vigilantes were blamed when convicted child molester William Malcolm – aka the Nightmare Man – got a nightmare of his own on 18 February 2000. He was shot dead when he answered the door of his second-floor flat in Manor Park, east London. The 47-year-old, who had two convictions for indecently assaulting children, was killed by a single bullet in the head. Neighbours heard a shot and rushed out to find him spreadeagled on the floor. Two stocky white men were seen fleeing the scene.

'His body was lying in the hallway,' said one woman. 'He had been shot in the head and there was blood pouring from him. He was still breathing but in a terrible state.'

An ambulance was called and Malcolm was rushed to the nearby Royal London Hospital but was pronounced dead on arrival.

Malcolm, a one-time army deserter, had been jailed in 1981 for the serial abuse of his six-year-old stepdaughter and nine-year-old stepson. When he was released from prison two years later, he was allowed to go back to live with the children and their mother. The attacks began again and in 1984 Malcolm went back to jail after being convicted of having unlawful intercourse with the stepdaughter he had abused before. The girl later revealed that Malcolm had begun abusing her at the age of three. The police then attempted to prosecute him again in 1994 on thirteen further child abuse charges, but an Old Bailey judge ruled that his previous convictions meant he could not get a fair trial. He was released, even though a psychiatric report described Malcolm as a sexual psychopath and said that he had paedophile tendencies of a 'strongly sadistic nature'.

As Malcolm was set free there were furious cries of 'kill the pervert' from the public gallery. The judge said it was with 'considerable regret' that he was forced to set Malcolm free and described the offences as 'unspeakable'.

Malcolm was an associate of the notorious paedophile Leslie 'Catweazle' Bailey. At one time, when Malcolm had been living with the five children, he would invite Bailey and others to join him as he tied the kids to their beds and abused them. One of the victims said later: 'He used to say he was not doing anything wrong and that if we told anyone he would take our mum away from us.'

Malcolm also intimidated his victims by boasting he

had been present at the killing of runaway rent boy Jason Swift, who was just fourteen when he died. Malcom's friendship with Bailey linked him to the paedophile ring led by Sidney Cooke; Robert Oliver and Lennie Smith were also associates. The gang tortured and murdered at least nine young boys, including Swift, seven-year-old Mark Tildesley and Barry Lewis, who was six. Detectives questioned Malcolm about the killings. Bailey was himself murdered in 1993, in top-security Whitemoor Prison, Cambridgeshire. Cooke and Oliver were paroled in 1998, and Smith in 1999. This case stirred up public anger, verging on hysteria, against actual and suspected child sex offenders. Across the country militant community organisations such as the Campaign against Paedophiles in Birmingham and the Unofficial Child Protection Unit in Glasgow sprung up to hunt down sex offenders. These shadowy unofficial groups name and shame those who are suspected, guilty or not, and then terrorise them.

In April 1998 protesters surrounded a police station in Bristol, believing it housed Sidney Cooke. A barrage of petrol bombs and bricks were thrown, leaving forty-six police officers injured as they tried to contain the crowd. Police said a peaceful protest had been hijacked by vigilantes. The rioters included children as young as eight.

Malcolm himself had provoked public outrage when it was revealed that he was among 600 convicted paedophiles whose movements were not being monitored because they had served their sentences before the compulsory Sex Offenders' Register had been introduced. Since then Malcolm had been the subject of repeated threats. After he was killed, the police investigated the idea that his murder was the work of vigilantes. It was possible that someone seeking summary justice had put a contract out on him. The shooting bore all the hallmarks of a professional 'hit'. A police source said: 'It was a classic hit – a knock on the door and he was shot. A lot of people will say he had it coming to him for what he has done to children in the past, but people cannot be allowed to take the law into their own hands.'

The killing came at the end of a week in which Britain was shocked by the sickening detail of the Welsh childcare scandal. It was revealed that some 650 children were victims of paedophiles, many of whom worked in the homes where the vulnerable youngsters were meant to be protected.

A child-protection cop said: 'The timing of the shooting in the same week the inquiry report into the North Wales children's homes was published may have been more than coincidence. The revulsion over the North Wales scandal could well have triggered it off.'

On the day of the killing the *Daily Mail* revealed that another police investigation was taking place into a nationwide network of paedophiles that had operated for over twenty years, on a scale which dwarfed the North Wales inquiry. At least one hundred paedophiles were thought to have been involved, and as many as 11,000 youngsters may have been abused. However, the newspaper warned: 'You can't take the law into your own hands.'

It seems someone did.

It was well known that Malcolm lived in Manor Park. Residents had been furious when he moved there, setting up home with new lover Donna Robinson and her three young children five years before. She was away from the flat when he was murdered. Local parents expressed alarm after it was discovered that he was working in a job opposite a cathedral school, having lied about his background when he applied for the post. Residents said they had known of his convictions and believed his death was a vigilante attack.

'There was a lot of trouble when he first moved here, then things died down,' said one man. 'You can't do what he did without creating an awful lot of enemies.'

Malcolm and his wife recently tried to move to nearby Canning Town but residents there blocked the move after learning of his crimes.

Neighbours expressed little sympathy over his death. One said: 'Nobody will feel sorry, except maybe his relatives. I was shocked when I heard someone had been shot on their doorstep like that, but when I heard it was him I was relieved.'

Another said: 'I won't be sending any flowers or shedding any tears. I don't think anyone will.'

The *Sun* called the killing an 'execution' and a mother living nearby said: 'His killers deserve a medal. Now my child will be able to walk the streets and play in safety. We're all relieved he is dead.'

'There will be no tears for him,' said 27-year-old Lorraine Webber as she cuddled her two-year-old daughter Chanynn May. 'It could not have happened to a nicer person. He should never have been allowed to live here in the first place amongst children.'

Another neighbour, 77-year-old Frank Lee, said: 'Killing Malcolm was the only cure for him. This area is full of vulnerable kids who play in the park opposite and in the streets. They will feel safer now.'

And a drinker at the nearby Blakesley Arms raised his glass and said: 'We will be dancing holes in our shoes tonight to celebrate this news. This is the best thing that could have happened to a bastard like that.'

Malcolm's former stepdaughter, whom he raped at the age of five, was glad at the news of his death.

Now 27, the woman, her two older sisters and two brothers had all suffered horrific abuse at the hands of Malcolm, whom they called "The Animal". She added: 'I'd love to meet the people who did it to say thank you – and buy them the biggest drink in the world.'

Still undergoing psychiatric counselling at the time of his death, she said: 'I've been jumping up and down with joy. Hearing "The Animal" was dead is the happiest I've ever felt.'

She still cannot bear to mention Malcolm's name.

'He wrecked my life,' she said. 'My daughter aged four is in care because I was unable to look after her properly. I'm trying to overcome a drink problem. I blame it on him.'

She also said that she knew she was a suspect in Malcolm's murder – as were her brothers and sisters. They were later interviewed by detectives.

'It was none of us,' she said, but insisted: 'I wish it *had* been me who killed him.'

Her sister, now a 40-year-old mother of four, said: 'Malcolm raped me when I was fourteen and did unspeakable things to me. When he walked away from the Old Bailey on a technicality I shouted out, "I hope you drop dead, you bastard." I am worried my family are going to get blamed for his murder.'

Malcolm's brother was also glad he was dead.

'I want to shake hands with his killers,' said father-of-four Andy Malcolm. 'He was vermin. I am glad he is dead … our entire family want to say how glad we are that Bill is no longer on this earth. As far as I am concerned my brother was lower than the rats in my barn.'

Brother Andy was living in France and said he wanted to break open champagne when one of his daughters phoned from England to say his paedophile brother had been shot dead.

'She said: "Have you heard – Bill got shot dead last night." I said: "Great, brilliant. We really need good news – we don't get much of it out here."'

He also received a call from the police. At the end of the call the officer said: 'Do you want to know anything if there are any developments?'

'Yes,' said Andy. 'When you catch the killers I want to come over there and shake their hands and say thank you very much. That is the reaction of the whole family. My mum loved him when she was alive and he was her son by some freak of nature. But as for the rest of us, it is good riddance. We are glad he is no longer on this earth.'

One of Malcolm's neighbours was eighteen-year-old Edmoses Theophile, whose younger brother Daniel Handley was kidnapped and murdered by two paedophiles while acting out their sexual fantasies. Nine-year-old Daniel was out riding his bike in 1994 when he was snatched by child abusers Brett Tyler and Timothy Morss. They took him to a south London flat and videotaped each other abusing the nine-year-old boy. Then they strangled him, dumping his body on the M4 as they drove towards Bristol.

The two men were told by the trial judge that 'life means life', but Theophile said: 'If I could, I would certainly kill them.'

He had lived next door to Malcolm for two years, but knew nothing of his criminal past. When he learnt of it, he said: 'I hope it's the beginning of a long line of executions.'

He also said he wanted the shooting to be seen as a 'blatant warning' for every paedophile.

'There's one less and I'm content with that fact,' he added. 'But there are still more out there. Some people can't sit back and wait for judgement day. Some people are going to make it themselves.'

However, another neighbour expressed concern about the murder. 'It's too extreme,' he said. 'Two wrongs don't make a right.'

Former Detective Chief Superintendent Roger Stoodley, who led the Operation Orchid investigation which nailed Cooke and Smith's gang, was also against vigilante action, saying that Malcolm should have been left to rot in jail.

'This would never have happened if Malcolm had been kept locked up in prison where he deserved to be,' he said. He later added that Malcolm 'deserved' to die because he was a convicted sex offender.

'I have no sympathy for him,' said Stoodley. 'How many times do we have to convict these people before something drastic happens?'

In a leading article, the *Sun* said: 'The hand-wringers care more about the rights of paedophiles than they do about the rights of children. Malcolm was clearly a sick, evil man. He should have been locked up for life, not just for society's protection but also for his own. If he had been in a secure prison where he belonged he could not have been shot. Vigilantes only operate when the system fails to properly punish or deter criminals ... It wasn't just the man who pulled the trigger who killed William Malcolm, it was the whole rotten bunch of lawyers and social workers who sent him back into society. They are as sick and perverted as he was.'

Sun readers wrote in to support the killers. One even suggested that they should be knighted. Others pointed out that nothing could justify a cold-blooded killing – the position the newspaper itself took. However, most agreed that the killers had only done what the courts had failed to do. Instead, vigilantes had stepped in with their own form of justice.

CHAPTER 9
SYMPATHY FOR THE DEVIL

The bloody corpse of 52-year-old Andrew Cunningham was found on 10 December 2008 in the dilapidated caravan where he lived alone on an industrial estate in Wandsworth, south-west London. A post-mortem examination gave the cause of death as multiple stab wounds to the head, neck and chest. The newspapers reported that his genitals had also been mutilated and police believe he may have been murdered by vigilantes. Cunningham was a convicted paedophile after having been jailed for four months in 2000 for unlawful sex with a fifteen-year-old girl.

However, another fifteen-year-old girl, who gave her name only as Lucy, laid a bunch of flowers near the dead man's caravan. She said that Cunningham was 'like a second dad' to her. A dedication on the flowers read: 'To Andy, the best man alive no matter what people say. Me and the family will miss you. May you rest in peace.'

Speaking for herself and her father, who is a deaf-mute,

she told reporters: 'Whoever did this was sick ... I used to go round his caravan instead of going to school. He never laid a finger on me. He told me to go back to school.'

Cunningham worked as a lorry driver for the Riverside Haulage company and lived on site at the Windmill Business Centre, where his body was discovered. Cunningham moved there after vigilantes had set fire to a bag of rubbish outside his former house in Wandsworth in 2003. This came after he was arrested and released without charge over further allegations he was grooming children for sex. Former neighbour 46-year-old Joe Hart said: 'He used to befriend young lads and invite them round, letting them do what they wanted in his house. He'd ask the boys to bring over girls and make passes at them.'

Other neighbours said Cunningham would regularly receive a 'hiding' from people who had heard these stories about him.

'He had lots of trouble,' said Lucy. 'He used to drink in one of the pubs, but there was a woman there who would always get into arguments with him, and somebody else stole his car.'

Lucy addressed those who had persecuted Cunningham in a handwritten note she left at the scene. It read: 'To those that hate. You may carry on hating.'

There were also words for their victim.

'There was no need for what happened to you. I have

known you most of my life and never have you laid a finger on me or my friends. You even met my boyfriend and it was a tragedy what happened. Me and the family will miss you! We all love you!'

Donald Findlater, of the child protection charity Lucy Faithfull Foundation, warned this type of vigilante attack could force other sex offenders into hiding.

'I completely understand why people do and should feel appalled by the harm that sex offenders cause, but members of the public taking the law into their own hands is not the way to deal with the situation,' he said.

It was thought the frenzied attack was the work of a group of young vigilantes. A passer-by claimed: 'I saw a group of about three or four kids hanging around that night. They were about sixteen or seventeen. They were trying to have a fight with someone and they were shouting, "Come here, come here." They were being very aggressive and looking at the caravan. When I saw them I just went away.'

Detectives said Cunningham may have known his killer or killers as there was no damage to his door, which he usually kept locked.

Shortly before his murder, drinkers at a nearby pub claimed that Cunningham had assaulted another girl. It was said that he had been molesting a barmaid's two-year-old daughter. Although this allegation was never reported to police, mobs reportedly drove past his caravan chanting: 'Die, paedo, die.'

The police source said that that Cunningham was loathed by a large number of people because of his paedophile past 'so we have a lot of potential suspects'. Detective Chief Inspector Nick Scola, leading the investigation, said: 'This was a vicious and brutal attack.' He added that people in the area 'knew about his history'.

'I heard it was a planned attack,' said 23-year-old Wazir Zadran, who worked at a nearby fish factory. 'Everyone knew he lived there and was a paedophile.'

According to Zadran, Cunningham hardly kept a low profile: 'I know he lived here and I used to hear him listening to the radio every night. It was always really loud, just blaring out music – I do not know any more than that.'

Another man who lived nearby said: 'I met him a couple of times. He was a really nice man, he offered to let me stay with him one night when I had nowhere to go, and when I didn't have any money he would give me food.'

However, one drinker in the Corner Pin, a pub less than fifty yards from the murder scene, showed no remorse.

'He was a nonce,' he said. 'Everybody around here knew it. I suppose there was some who felt he had it coming.'

Cunningham had been dogged for years by taunts. There were even reports that firebombers had targeted his caravan.

Cunningham's body had been found by his employer, who said: 'He had a stab wound in his neck and there was blood everywhere. The bed was soaked and his head was lying in it. He was a nice bloke as far as I know, this is a complete shock.'

He admitted, however, that he did not know Cunningham well. 'The less you know about drivers the better – you do not want to get involved,' he said. 'He phoned me up and asked if he could drive for me. He'd worked for me before so I gave him a job.' He said he had no idea about his employee's criminal past. 'He was a lovely man, he couldn't do enough for me.'

However, his sympathy was far from universal. One van driver passing the murder scene shouted: 'He deserved it.'

Police said the 2000 incident was Mr Cunningham's only conviction for sexual offences, and he came off the Sex Offenders' Register in March.

Detective Chief Inspector Scola said: 'Regardless of who he was or what he may have done, Andrew was the victim of a vicious assault which ended his life.'

Cunningham had five children and was estranged from a former partner.

'He moved out of his house after his relationship with the mother of his children broke up,' said Lucy. 'He was very open about why he went to prison. He said it was a misunderstanding. He said he wanted to be left alone to get on with his life in his caravan.'

But his ex was less forgiving.

'He's had what was coming to him,' she said, branding him 'pure, cold evil'.

'No one should feel sorry for him,' she insisted. 'I know mob justice is wrong but he caused a lot of innocent kids a lot of unimaginable pain.'

Her contempt was echoed by one of the couple's daughters, who was 22 at the time of his death.

'I want to spit on his grave,' she said. 'He will always be my dad. I hate him for everything he did to me but no one should be murdered in such cold blood. I lay awake all night wondering whether he was dead or alive when they tried to castrate him – if it was quick or if he suffered.'

Another of Cunningham's daughters blasted his killers, saying: 'I hope whoever did this gets the same kind of violent end.'

Sara Payne – mother of eight-year-old daughter Sarah whose murder by a paedophile sparked the *News of the World*'s name-and-shame campaign – also condemned the vigilante killers of Andrew Cunningham. She said it was a blow to her hopes of a 'Sarah's Law', which would alert families to child sex offenders living in their midst.

'Every time someone like Cunningham is attacked,' she said, 'it gives paedophiles another reason to remain anonymous. Those who feel strongly about active paedophiles have only one option: go to the police.

Men like Cunningham belong in the dock of the Old Bailey – not a hospital morgue.'

In June 2009 viewers of BBC's *Crimewatch* were asked to identify one of the suspected killers of Andrew Cunningham by his laughter. His cackle was captured on CCTV near Cunningham's caravan the night he was murdered, though the killers' faces could not be seen.

'Someone may recognise who it is,' said Detective Chief Inspector Scola. 'Whoever it is can be heard having a conversation and then there are two high-pitched laughs.'

So far no progress has been reported in the case. Perhaps the police have met another wall of silence, as so often happens when they investigate attacks on paedophiles, who are usually universally despised. However, it appears that Andrew Cunningham was a special case. Lucy's was not the only bunch of flowers left at the murder scene. One came with a note that read: 'To Andy, the best man alive, no matter what people say.'

A week after Cunningham's body was found, the police began another murder investigation after a blood-drenched room was found in Padiham, Lancashire. Officers feared 26-year-old convicted rapist Alan Lee Street had been tortured and hacked to death by vigilantes. Neighbours heard screaming and the police arrived to find a huge pool of blood. It was clear that no victim could survive such massive blood loss, although the corpse had been removed. Street's body was found a month later near Accrington and four men were charged with his murder.

CHAPTER 10
PUNISHING THE GUILTLESS

A man in a wheelchair was attacked by a vigilante gang led by a registered nurse at his home in Liskeard, Cornwall. They were looking for the disabled man's brother, a suspected paedophile. The nurse, 59-year-old Peter Hartley of Colne, Lancashire, had been out drinking with the disabled man's father in August 2006 when the father told him that one of his sons had allegedly molested his daughter and another young girl. The two men, accompanied by their girlfriends, went to see the disabled son to find out where his brother was. The 47-year-old invalid suffered from motor neurone disease and was recovering from a stroke at the time.

They broke into his house and when he wouldn't – or couldn't – tell them where his brother was, they attacked him, hitting him with a spatula and a picture frame. Hartley punched him, breaking his nose and knocking him to the ground. Then the invalid's own father kicked him as he lay motionless on the floor.

Hartley never fully admitted to punching the man

and also claimed he was restraining the other three. Nevertheless, he was convicted at Liskeard magistrates' court of assault by beating and using threatening, abusive or insulting words. He was fined £450. He was also ordered to pay £385 in compensation and £34 in costs.

Hartley has since been struck off the professional register as a nurse. The chairwoman of the Nursing and Midwifery Council said: 'This was a most serious case of vigilante action by an alcohol-fuelled group causing serious injury to a particularly vulnerable and entirely innocent victim.'

Gordon Buchanan, 54, was targeted by vigilantes after allowing his friend of twenty years, paedophile rock star Gary Glitter, to stay in his two-million-pound home in Hampshire when Glitter returned from Vietnam after spending nearly three years in jail there for abusing two girls. However, after four days, Glitter's bolthole was discovered after he went shopping in Warsash, near Southampton. He was recognised even though he had shaved off his distinctive beard and donned a ginger wig. Glitter was whisked off to a new hideaway paid for by the authorities.

'It must be costing millions,' Buchanan said. 'After he was discovered at my house, six police cars escorted us out of Hampshire. We needed petrol and they closed a whole petrol station just for the two of us. It was a massive police operation. I can't begin to think how much it must have cost. And the cost will keep going up because it's only a matter of time before Gary's new hideout is discovered and the whole thing will be repeated again at vast expense to the taxpayer.'

Despite everything, Buchanan remained true to his old friend. He believed that Glitter was a schizophrenic and arranged for psychiatrist and child abuse specialist Dr Valerie Sinason to fly from South Africa to treat his pal.

'He needs psychiatric help,' said Buchanan. 'He needs to be in hospital.'

But while Glitter was protected by the full might of the law, Buchanan was left vulnerable to attack by vigilantes.

He said: 'My decision to offer him sanctuary has ruined my life.'

Gary Glitter may be guilty of paedophilia, but Buchanan was guilty of nothing but loyalty.

Although no one was caught in the Glitter–Buchanan case, two men were jailed after attacking a neighbour they wrongly accused of being a paedophile. Thomas Powch, 44, and William Ross, 38, made a vigilante attack on 37-year-old James Brown with a makeshift flamethrower after another resident of their block told them he had been looking at children. The two had originally accused another man of being a paedophile in Greendykes Road, Edinburgh, in April 2008. When they were told they had the wrong address, Powch and Ross went to Brown's flat in the same block at 10 a.m. and accused him of being a 'beast' and a 'paedophile'. Brown denied their allegations, so Ross punched him twice, knocking him to the floor.

Father-of-six Ross then said, 'This is how you treat scum.'

He grabbed an aerosol can of Brut deodorant and sprayed it in Brown's face while Powch lit the vapour with a cigarette lighter. They dumped the can into Brown's lap and left. Brown suffered burns to his face, neck and hair, but escaped serious injury. He moved out of his apartment the following day and was homeless for some time.

Powch and Ross were charged with attempted murder, but pleaded guilty to the lesser charge of assault. Defence counsel Stephen Mannifield said Ross, who was on bail at the time, had been drinking heavily before the attack and later regretted acting on false information. Powch's lawyer, Leanne McQuillan, said her client suffered alcohol problems and was ashamed of having listened to the rumours.

'A third party had a grievance with the victim and he imparted certain information to Mr Powch,' she said. 'He foolishly acted on this.'

Sentencing them at Edinburgh sheriff court, Sheriff Derrick McIntyre said: 'This vigilante-type assault took place in a stranger's home in the morning. You had both been drinking. He was injured, surprisingly not seriously, but he was afraid to leave his flat and has trouble sleeping.'

The men were jailed for two years.

A former soldier from Onllwyn in South Wales, who was cleared of attempting to rape a young girl, spent three days in hospital after being attacked by a gang of vigilantes. Gwyn Rowlands, 28, was walking home from a night out with his girlfriend when they were set upon. Rowlands suffered a swelling of the brain after the assault. His girlfriend was also hurt.

Rowlands had been accused of raping an underage girl. He strenuously denied all knowledge of the offence, but had to put plans to join the prison service and get married on hold because of the case. When the case came to trial, he was cleared by Swansea Crown court.

'I had already gone through hell with the court case hanging over me,' he said. 'The day I was cleared in court, I was so relieved because there had been so much pressure on myself and my family for nearly a year.'

But the relief was short-lived. He had been out with his girlfriend at a pub in nearby Banwen when a group of men started taunting him, calling him a paedophile, before assaulting him.

'I was hit to the floor and while I was down one of them decided to stamp on me and then kick and punch me,' said Rowlands. 'My girlfriend got thrown to the ground and she ended up with bruises and grazes to her knees and elbows. I ended up in hospital with a swelling to my brain.'

In defence of her son, his mother Jan Rowlands turned to a little vigilante action of her own. She posted an open letter to 370 homes in her son's neighbourhood in the Dulais Valley, emphasising his innocence and denouncing his assailants as 'mindless morons'. She also thanked those people who had not turned their backs on her son.

'I spent three days in Morriston Hospital,' he said, 'but I still haven't recovered – I get dizzy spells.'

Rowlands had already spent seven years with the army, but signed up again and moved away from Onllwyn with his young family to escape any further run-ins with the vigilantes.

'It's a relief and a disappointment,' he said. 'I want a fresh start for us, so we can put all this behind us. But it's disappointing because I have lived in this house for eight years and we had got it just the way we wanted it.'

His mother told the press: 'Even though he is totally innocent, some mindless morons have decided that the court is wrong and that the jury were incorrect in their findings.'

His attackers have yet to be caught.

A vigilante knifeman, Reuben Atkinson, attacked an

80-year-old pensioner in north Tyneside after being told he was a child molester. Atkinson walked into the pensioner's home through an unlocked door in the middle of the morning and said, 'I'm going to kill you.'

He also demanded money and the victim gave him twenty pounds. Then Atkinson pulled a kitchen knife from his pocket and chased the pensioner towards the back door.

'He was caught by the defendant who held the knife towards him and tried to stab him in the front of the body,' said prosecutor Stephen Duffield at Newcastle Crown court. 'The victim put up his hands to try to protect himself and there was a struggle.'

The pensioner received cuts to his index finger and wrist, but managed to get out of the door. However, the police had already been tipped off and had rung him to warn Atkinson was on his way. They were on the phone when the assailant broke in. By the time the pensioner made his escape, an armed response squad was on its way. Cornered by the police, Atkinson dropped the knife, but continued shouting: 'He's a paedophile. I'm going to kill him.'

Police investigated Atkinson's accusations and decided no further action should be taken.

Defence counsel Tom Moran said six-footer Atkinson, who was 42, could easily have used his height and weight to overpower the pensioner.

'When it came to the crunch and when he could

have caused very serious harm or even killed him, he did not,' he said.

The pensioner had been treated in hospital for minor injuries to his hand and arm.

'This was a wicked attack on a vulnerable 80-year-old man and whatever reason you gave it was entirely unjustified,' said Recorder Graham Hyland. 'You chose to take the law in your own hands. It was a premeditated attack with the use of a knife.'

Although he gave Atkinson credit for pleading guilty to unlawful wounding, he jailed him for three years.

'It has to be a lengthy prison term,' he said.

Graham Partington, a disabled former labourer, lived under siege on an estate in Manchester for three months after his son, 20, was wrongly accused of child abuse. Petrol bombs were hurled through the windows. Rocks were thrown. Partington's fourteen-year-old daughter had wood varnish poured into her hair and, eventually, their home was looted by people they once thought of as their friends.

The intimidation came to a head in July 1997, when a gang of sixty men and women gathered around their door chanting 'beast' and 'pervert'.

'We were afraid to go to sleep in case the mob broke in,' said Partington. 'The following day we thought things had calmed down when a stone smashed through the window and hit my ten-year-old daughter, which was the final straw. We left, and two days later the house was looted and all our belongings, such as our wedding and birth certificates, were burnt.'

Partington was forced to find refuge in a homeless shelter with his wife and five children.

But the vigilantes were unrepentant. One nineteen-year-old, who admitted throwing bricks at the Partington house, said: 'They are just scum. I don't regret what I did for a moment. I pity whoever has to live next to them when the council finally gives them a new house.'

A 24-year-old man was abducted by vigilantes in the Midlands in March 2000, according to the *Guardian*. They beat and tortured him for a week, believing him to be a paedophile. Its sister newspaper, the *Manchester Evening News*, was implicated in an attack on 67-year-old Francis Duffy, who suffers from senile dementia. Duffy was beaten and severely injured by vigilantes after being mistaken for a paedophile, Brynley Dummett, who had been named by the *Evening News* in a warning to residents of the Ancoats housing estate that a convicted child molester was living in their midst. Dummett, who had six convictions for sex offences, had been driven out of the estate and moved to Chorlton-on-Medlock, also in Manchester, where local women visited schools and houses, distributing copies of his picture. A mob went in search of Dummett. Instead they found Francis Duffy who bore some physical resemblance to the sex offender. He was battered to the ground by several women and suffered a broken wrist, a broken finger and severe bruising. After the attack on Duffy, Dummett fled. The police said they had no knowledge of his whereabouts. Michael Unger, the editor of the *Manchester Evening News*, accepted no responsibility for the incident.

In Reading, a burglar who was made to wear a tagging device was attacked by a gang after a media story that a sex offender in the town had been made to wear a similar tag; while in the west Midlands, a fourteen-year-old girl was killed when her home was firebombed in an arson attack intended for a paedophile.

In 1997, in Folkestone, Kent, 55-year-old Frank Revill was targeted by vigilantes who falsely believed he was a paedophile. Word had spread that a child abuser was due to move into his neighbourhood. Then Revill was spotted moving things into a house belonging to his daughter.

'The vigilantes saw me, put two and two together and got five,' he said.

Revill was verbally abused. The windows of his daughter's house were smashed and he received threatening phone calls.

'The thought of paedophiles abhors me,' he told the *Sunday Times*, 'but at the other extreme, vigilantes should be stopped from taking the law into their own hands.'

Revill had been mistaken for a paedophile named in posters put up around the area.

'People need this information but it has to be done properly,' he said. 'It only takes one nut to put a lighted rag through the door.'

That October, 40-year-old Ralph Lowe from Bingley, Yorkshire, was puzzled when normally friendly neighbours shunned him as he went out for a walk. Later that day he discovered that a group calling itself the Council for the Protection of Children had identified him as an alleged child molester in a leaflet circulated to all his neighbours. After that he was threatened by passers-by and a brick was thrown through his window. He said: 'I think I am the victim of a smear campaign by someone I know. It is worrying that some madman who sees that leaflet could kill me because they think I am a pervert.' Police and local children's organisations confirmed that Lowe was not a sex offender. Lowe was uninjured, but, in another case of mistaken identity, 48-year-old James Cameron from Kilmarnock was permanently disabled after he was mistakenly implicated as a child sex abuser. He was stabbed in the hand and face and had petrol poured over him by two attackers who believed he had abused one of their friends.

*

A couple in Dundee and their three grandchildren were denied a house in Kirkton after vigilantes warned their lives would be in danger if they moved in. The vigilante group wrongly believed that one of the family was a paedophile and agents renting the house were bombarded with threatening phone calls. Even though it was a case of mistaken identity, the agents cancelled the rental agreement the day before the family were due to be given the keys, saying that giving them the house would put them in danger.

'We are all upset with the situation because the family are decent people trying to piece back their lives and upon processing them as probable tenants we received threatening phone calls,' said Mark Taylor of Taylor Housing. 'We sadly felt that to give them a house in Kirkton would place them in immediate danger and so had no choice but to deny them a tenancy. We aim to provide decent homes to decent people and a situation such as this saddens us because this poor family are still being subjected to awful abuse.'

Elaine Stenson of Dundee Property Management who handled tenancies for Taylor Housing said: 'We took three phone calls expressing their concerns as residents of the area. They made clear in no uncertain terms not to put the family into that house or there would be trouble. We were left with no option but to contact the family and Mark Taylor immediately. Taylor Housing decided they could not house them because of health and safety concerns.'

Again Mrs Stenson said she was in absolutely no doubt that it was a case of mistaken identity.

'It's started off as a malicious rumour that has had devastating consequences,' she said. 'The people of Kirkton have shamefully made threats without finding out the facts. Is this how Dundee wishes to be portrayed?'

Twenty-four-year-old Marc Paul Smith, from Stainforth, made a vigilante attack on a fourteen-year-old boy he wrongly suspected of vandalism. He attacked the boy with a golf club when he thought the teenager had broken a window at his home. A court was told that Smith was no thug but was driven to do what he did because he was haunted by the death of his 52-year-old grandfather Ernest Woodward who died after chasing vandals.

'Marc reacted because vandalism is a sensitive issue in our family,' said his aunt Michelle Tierney. 'My dad, Marc's grandfather, died twenty years ago in January after he collapsed and had a heart attack chasing a vandal. Someone had thrown a stone at the window. He chased him and he collapsed and died after chasing him about four hundred yards ... Our Marc and my daughter were only four and five at the time. They were always with him and were brought up with the trauma. Marc had never been in trouble before he was jailed.

Our family will not tolerate vandalism because of what happened to my dad. It has been a big thing in our lives. We feel Dad went before his time because of a vandal.'

The family said there was an ongoing problem with vandalism in Stainforth – but no one should take the law into their own hands.

'Taking the law into your own hands is not the way to go about it, whatever you may feel, and what happened to Marc is proof of that,' said Tierney.

Smith was jailed for three and half years.

The police feared that vigilante attacks would be made on 24-year-old Pat Williams after rumours spread through her village in South Wales that she was the girlfriend of Soham murderer Ian Huntley. Gossip spread that Maxine Carr, who had provided a false alibi for the child killer after the murders of ten-year-olds Holly Wells and Jessica Chapman, had been rehoused in Ystradgynlais and was secretly working in an art shop in the Swansea Valley. Williams's life quickly became unbearable and she considered leaving the village where she had lived for three years. She was pregnant at the time.

'It was really malicious and I was pretty upset, to tell you the truth,' she said. 'It made my life difficult. It made me want to move away. I started looking for places – anywhere other than here. Some people actually believed that I was her. Others didn't. But it was really spiteful.'

Carr herself had been hounded out of a Welsh town five years earlier after locals had discovered she had been rehoused there. Carr had pleaded guilty to perverting the course of justice in 2001 and was sentenced to five years. Released after serving twenty-one months in jail, she changed her appearance and was given a new identity. Nevertheless, it has been reported that Carr has been moved around the UK on several occasions after being recognised.

Pat Williams, who had a six-year-old daughter and another on the way, said she believed the rumour was started by a woman who got into an argument with a work colleague of hers.

'I was working in a shop as a cleaner at the time and people were spreading these rumours that I was Maxine Carr,' she said. 'When I went up to the woman who had spread the rumours and told her I wasn't her, she didn't apologise and just said that I looked like her. I wasn't in the mood to ask why she had done it. My husband Simon wasn't happy about it either.'

Pat Williams was a redhead and had a hairstyle similar to Carr's in the pictures issued at the time of her trial. But otherwise, she said: 'I don't think I have a resemblance to her.'

Nevertheless, a passing similarity to Carr was enough

to bring Welsh vigilantes down on her head, though other locals remained unconvinced.

'Some people said she looked a bit like her but the only picture I have seen of Maxine Carr is probably ten years old now,' said one resident of Ystrad. 'I had heard a lot of different stories but I didn't believe it was her.'

The atmosphere became so heated that a second shop in Ystradgynlais – which also sells some art – had also become a target. Pat Williams became so distressed about the gossip that she called the police. But this presented them with something of a dilemma. Court orders prevent Carr's new name and address being published and under police guidelines they are not allowed to confirm or deny her whereabouts. However, Dyfed–Powys Police became so concerned about the threat of vigilante action against Williams that they were forced to act to quell the rumours.

'I had images in my head of people taking the law into their own hands because it is still a very sensitive issue,' said Inspector Mark Davies. 'After completing all the necessary background checks, I took the view as a senior officer that the best way I could put the stories to bed was to talk to people in the village and let them know it was not correct. It was obviously a very distressing time for the young girl involved, who was a Swansea Valley girl born and bred.'

Another Ystrad resident explained: 'We are a small community so rumours can go around pretty quickly, especially when it is about something as serious as that. I'd heard the police had been into a few shops and told people it was definitely not true.'

But technology was on the side of the vigilantes. Users of social networking site Facebook had fuelled the speculation with postings by people in the group calling itself 'I've tracked down Maxine Carr!' They claimed that she is living in Coelbren, which is also in the Swansea Valley. *Wales on Sunday* said at least three women in the valley have been falsely accused of being Carr.

'People should be very careful before spreading these types of rumours because the consequences can be very serious,' said Inspector Davis.

Vigilante attacks based on false accusations are commonplace. Richard Clark, from Rothbury, Northumberland, took the law into his own hands on 23 December 2009 after being told that Terence Nichol had been questioned by police over the break-in at his late great-uncle Dick Murray's home. Armed with a pool cue, the 23-year-old kitchen porter went to 46-year-old Nichol's home to confront him. When Nichol answered the door, Clark smashed him over the head with the cue, sending him crashing to the ground.

Clark later pleaded guilty to assault at Alnwick magistrates' court. The prosecutor, James Long, said: 'The victim said the defendant raised the cue above his head and then struck him with great force, causing him to fall backwards into the hall. He then went into the house where he struck the victim again, continually abusing him saying he was the person who burgled the house.'

At one point, Nichol managed to grab the cue to defend himself, but Clark then punched him before fleeing the scene. In hospital, Nichol was treated for lacerations to the head.

When Clark was arrested, he admitted the assault. He said he had been drinking and playing pool at the Railway Hotel when he was told that Nichol had been questioned over the break-in at his great-uncle's house.

'Mr Clark was aware of the burglary and was told by a reliable person that this man was responsible,' said solicitor Steven Davis in Clark's defence. 'He was very angry, so he decided to have it out with the injured party and went to the house, but says that as the man came out he was drunk and aggressive.'

Clark denied hitting Nichol five times, as the prosecution had suggested. Instead he said he had only hit Nichol with the cue twice. No police action was ever taken against Mr Nichol, who maintained his innocence throughout. Following the attack, he suffered from Post Concussion Syndrome.

Since the attack, Clark said he had recognised the severity of his actions and was 'sickened' at what he had done. He was convicted of causing actual bodily harm and was sentenced to carry out a twelve-month community order with seventy-five hours of unpaid work. Clark was also order to pay Nichol £100 compensation and £70 court costs.

But vigilante action does not always lead to violence. Forty-seven-year-old vigilante Colin Haw filmed gay men meeting up for sex in the wood near Sleaford in Lincolnshire and posted the footage on a website in an attempt to name and shame. The father of two said he reported the problem to the police but was ignored, so he decided to take action as the area was visited by families and children.

The self-employed mechanic formed a vigilante group who wore balaclavas and combat kit, and carried a video camera and walkie-talkies. Calling themselves 'undercover agents', members of the group waited by lay-bys in the Sleaford area, telling motorists they were 'officers' carrying out 'surveillance'. Sometimes they would pretend to be looking for sex to lure gay men into the area before confronting them on camera. Haw then posted the footage on the popular website www.bostontown.net, which recorded 9.2 million hits between January 2008 and April 2009. The video footage was given a soundtrack using the songs such as 'YMCA' by the Village People and the nursery rhyme 'The Teddy Bears' Picnic'. The men featured were also given derogatory names. As a result, Haw himself was arrested.

The prosecutor Stephen Hill told Boston magistrates' court of the experience of a motorcyclist who he said feared what was going to happen when he was confronted in the area and wondered whether the group was going to stab him.

Defence counsel Liz Harte admitted that Haw's action was a 'misguided enterprise'. But she said: 'There were several people involved and one or two of them raised this matter with police. The fact of the matter was that nothing was done about it. That's why some people engaged in this vigilante activity. In this aspect, Mr Haw thought he was doing the right thing. The thinking was that he was a protector of morals and a guardian of children.'

However, she added: 'Vigilante activity can never be acceptable.'

Haw, of Mayflower Road, Boston, earlier admitted a public order offence for filming one of his victims in a lay-by next to the A17 on 17 June 2008. Chairman of the bench Pat Walsh told Haw: 'Your actions were premeditated and quite deliberate in targeting a group of people we would describe as vulnerable. Our thoughts were to send you to custody but we are not going to do that today.'

He sentenced Haw to four months in prison, suspended for a year and a half. He also ordered him to do two hundred hours' unpaid community service work and gave him an eighteen-month supervision order. On top of that he had to pay the motorcyclist £400 compensation and was ordered to pay £120 costs. However, the magistrate rejected Lincolnshire Police's application for an antisocial behaviour order.

In an impromptu press conference outside court, Haw said: 'We didn't go in there to cause people harm. We reported it on several occasions to the police. We tried to name and shame them but we didn't have any intention of causing them distress. We didn't put up any pornographic material.'

He claimed that he had become an amateur filmmaker in the public interest and that previous footage posted on the website had done good.

'In our videos in Boston we have also brought attention to all the rubbish and the drug users who have thrown their syringes on the floor,' he said. 'We were not out to cause any trouble. The police wanted it covered up. I've got nothing against homosexual people, but what gives them the authority to do it in public?'

Women are sometimes the worst offenders when it comes to vigilante action. On 15 May 2008, 38-year-old Tracey Ann Campbell approached a man suffering from cerebral palsy as he left a police station in Newton Aycliffe in a motorised wheelchair and accused him of being a child molester. Durham Crown court heard that she smelt strongly of alcohol when she bent down to make the accusation directly into his face. Graeme Gaston, prosecuting, said the disabled man responded by slapping her cheek, but she then punched him three times, scratched his face and attempted to poke her thumbs into his eyes. She also kicked him up to four times in the face, leaving him with bruises and lacerations around his eyes, face and nose.

'When it came to an end, he went straight back to report the attack at the police station,' said Gaston.

The police said that Campbell was still smelling strongly of drink when she was arrested nearby. She told officers: 'I hate people like that.'

Richard Herrmann, mitigating, said his client thought the complainant made a comment to her, to which she responded.

'She thought this man was a known offender and she admits being prejudiced,' he said. Campbell 'expresses a loathing of sex offenders', having previously remonstrated at the home of another man, Herrmann added.

'She seems to be a one-woman posse of vigilantes,' commented Recorder David Gordon.

Campbell, of Bridge Street, Howden-le-Wear, near Crook, admitted assault causing actual bodily harm. She was jailed for nine months.

Some vigilantes go to extraordinary lengths. Three travelled a hundred miles to seek revenge – only to end up beating up the wrong man. The Tyneside gang drove from Newcastle to Lincolnshire, but when they realised they'd bungled the job, they got lost and finally broke down on the A1 as they headed back to the north-east. They then abandoned the getaway car and their weapons, but the police tracked them down using finger-prints and DNA. Terry Simpson, of Granville Road, Jesmond, Newcastle, and John Ash, of Half Moon Lane, Gateshead, were arrested, along with Lisa Wheatley, of Hendon Valley, Sunderland, who was Ash's daughter.

Lincoln Crown court heard how the group headed for Louth, Lincolnshire, in November 2007. Their target there was Mark Scotter. They alleged that he had sent abusive text messages to Wheatley, who was his step-daughter.

John Dee, prosecuting, said Wheatley's father Ash decided to 'deal' with Scotter and recruited 'hired goons'.

'They were armed with a crowbar, hammer and pepper spray but went to the wrong address,' Dee said.

As a result, Mr Scotter's neighbour Alan Petch was attacked in his home. The 59-year-old was pepper-sprayed in his face. But the terrified man pleaded with his attackers, who fled after one of them shouted 'that's not Scotter'.

Dee said the incident had changed Petch's life. 'Even in daytime he now looks out of the window to see who is there,' he said.

Police later linked Simpson to the bungled raid when his DNA was found on a crowbar and hammer abandoned by the side of the car on the A1. Ash, 44, Simpson, 32, and Wheatley, 24, all pleaded guilty to conspiring to assault Scotter. Ash and Simpson also admitted assault causing actual bodily harm.

Judge Michael Heath told them: 'You decided on some vigilante attack to sort Mr Scotter out. What happened illustrates what happens when people take the law into their own hands. A wholly innocent man who lived next door to Mr Scotter was attacked in his own home.'

Simpson, who had a string of previous convictions for assault, was jailed for three years. Ash was sentenced to two and a half years in prison, while mother-of-four Wheatley was given a sentence of fifty-one weeks, suspended for a year.

Another vigilante gang admitted driving from Merseyside to Gwynedd armed with baseball bats looking for a man they thought was a rapist. The gang of four pulled up in Blaenau Ffestiniog and accosted a man and woman walking on the pavement. The man fled, but the woman was seized and slapped across the face by the gang who demanded that she tell them where the man would be hiding.

However, witnesses had seen the car screech to a halt and called the police, giving them the car's registration number. It was later stopped in Bala. When the car was searched, police found three baseball bats and a balaclava-style ski mask in the boot. The accused told police they had been given the nickname of a person living in Blaenau Ffestiniog who had allegedly raped a family member. In fact, the gang had picked on the wrong man who had nothing to do with any allegations of rape.

Giselle Cooper, 22, Aaron Cooper, 25, of Powder Road, Rock Ferry, and Marie Moore, 36, of Woodward Road, Rock Ferry, and a seventeen-year-old youth, unnamed for legal reasons, had all pleaded guilty to possessing offensive weapons. Cooper also pleaded guilty to common assault on the unnamed woman while the seventeen-year-old pleaded guilty to threatening behaviour against the unnamed man. They were given community service orders. The baseball bats and balaclavas were confiscated.

A far more brutal assault took place on an eccentric neighbour in Leeds. David Bigsby and Michael McDonald burst into Gregory McGrath's Scarborough home while he was asleep and began beating him with a baseball bat and a metal bar. McGrath suffered multiple injuries, including a fractured cheekbone, broken elbow and extensive bruising over his face, arms, legs and body. The police and an ambulance crew found him lying face down in a pool of blood. He complained of problems breathing, and when he was taken to hospital was found to be bleeding internally into the chest cavity.

Sixty-year-old McGrath was known as an eccentric character who had alcohol and mental health problems, and neighbours had made complaints to the police about him in the past. Bigsby, 33, had had a number of run-ins with McGrath and a case was pending before magistrates in which McGrath allegedly threatened him with a rolling-pin. Unhappy with the way the police had handled the situation Bigsby decided to take the matter into his own hands and recruited the help of 43-year-old McDonald. They had been drinking together when they decided to beat up McGrath.

At Leeds Crown court, Judge Scott Wolstenholme said Mr McGrath might have been a 'troublesome neighbour' whom they considered a danger to their families, but 'that doesn't begin to excuse what happened when you both decided to take the law into your own hands.'

Bigsby had made previous threats concerning McGrath. He had even told the police that McGrath was a pervert and deserved everything he got. He said he was tired of the problems he had had with McGrath whom he considered was provoking him. McDonald said he had heard that McGrath had been exposing himself to young people and accepted that he had been drinking when he agreed to go along that evening. The two men were jailed for six years.

Another three vigilantes who kidnapped and threatened to kill a man they believed had stolen from them were also jailed. Vitalijs Lizunovs, Andrejs Terehovs and Aleksandrs Filatovs bundled their victim into the boot of a car and drove him to the side of a canal in Goole, Humberside, where they threatened to drown him. Hull Crown court was told that the three men bound the legs of victim, twenty-year-old Lithuanian Artiom Galimov, with cling film and said they were going to tie a stone to him and throw him in the canal near Bridge Street.

The court heard the victim was walking past Jefferson Street at about 8.30 p.m. on 23 January when he was grabbed by 27-year-old Lizunovs and his eighteen-year-old nephew Filatovs, of Malvern Road. They grabbed his arms and forced him back against a wall and said: 'You are going with us.'

He resisted, saying that he did not want to go with them because he was scared they wanted to hit him.

'One of them said, "No, we want to stab you," and he fell to the ground to try and thwart his attackers,' Mark Kendall, prosecuting, told the court.

Terehovs, 27, of Dunhill Road, then seized the victim by the collar and the three men began dragging him towards Jefferson Street. A witness saw them pushing him and kicking him on the ground, then he was taken to a Volkswagen Passat and forced into the boot. The victim said he was in the car for about five minutes before the boot was opened. The three men, who were from Latvia, then threatened to wrap him in plastic and throw him in the canal. They accused him of being involved in a burglary at Lizunovs' home, and asked him to give Lizunovs' possessions back. Eventually, they relented and gave him a cigarette before driving off and leaving him by the canal.

Police were alerted by CCTV operators who had seen part of the incident. They stopped the assailants' car at about 8.45 p.m. on Carlisle Street. Terehovs admitted what they had done but said they had only done it because he had stolen from them. The men then pointed out their victim to the officers.

No evidence was found to support their claim that Galimov had been involved in the burglary and none of the stolen items was recovered.

Sentencing the three men, Judge Roger Thorn, QC, said: 'It is a feature of all civilisations throughout the world that the rule of law applies. It was not for any of you to become vigilantes, to take the law into your own hands. You must realise that in these circumstances I have no option but to send all three of you to custody.'

Lizunovs and Terehovs were sentenced to three years and four months in prison and Filatovs was jailed for two and a half years.

*

Forty-three-year-old dad Andrew Langley went into hiding after vigilante letters branding him a 'sick paedophile' were posted through neighbours' letter boxes in Lincoln. The letter said he had molested a six-year-old girl.

'This sick individual has been driven out of two failed relationships for the same reasons of being caught collecting and exchanging child pornography,' it went on.

Police visited his house on the afternoon of 17 July 2007 to tell him what was happening. After their visit he said he considered suicide. He went for a long walk, only returning at 5.30 the following morning. From then on, he sat in his living room with the curtains drawn and the television turned off. He put an extra lock on his door. Terrified at what could happen to him, he packed his bags ready to flee the city that has been his home for twenty-seven years.

'I've known some of the neighbours for years but now I can't face them – I mean, what would I say to them?' said Langley, who had been unable to work for several years through stress. 'I was lost for words after reading the letter. I fear for my life now and have no choice but to leave. In everybody's eyes I am a paedophile regardless of what the truth is. I've become paranoid now because everyone who walks past my home seems to look in. It's not fair on my neighbours either – they shouldn't have to go through all this.'

Langley denied all of the allegations and said he would press charges against the person who wrote the letter defaming him. Lincolnshire Police confirmed that the allegations were untrue and said that the letter was being treated as malicious.

'Our advice is to ignore the letter. We've spoken to people who are concerned about it, but the letter seems to be unfounded,' said police spokesman Dick Holmes. 'Letters like these can in extreme cases lead to violence and disorder and they make the life of the person targeted very uncomfortable. We are now launching an investigation into who sent the letters.'

Neighbours in De Wint Avenue and nearby streets were shocked when they received the letter. But while the police told them to ignore the allegations, they quickly became a talking point.

Margaret Wright, a 49-year-old mental health worker who lived in nearby Constable Close, expressed her disgust that such rumours should be spread.

'It's absolutely sick,' she said. 'The poor man will have to live with that for the rest of his life. People could smash his house up or anything – no innocent person deserves that. I can't imagine being accused of anything worse.'

Another neighbour said: 'I find it rather distasteful to send letters like this about people. Those reading it have no idea how much evidence there is against the

CHAPTER 11
SLAUGHTER OF
THE INNOCENTS

Vigilantes do not just ostracise and assault those they believe, wrongly, of serious offences. Sometimes they murder. On 18 March 2006, 42-year-old Paul Cooper was found dead in his flat in Heywood, Greater Manchester. Wrongly accused of being a paedophile, he had been stabbed to death in a brutal and prolonged attack.

'There is no evidence to suggest that Paul was ever involved in any sexual offence,' said Detective Chief Inspector Jeff McMahon.

Neil Read, 23, of Higher Lomax Lane in Heywood, was arrested in connection with the crime, but at Manchester Minshull Street Crown court he was deemed unfit to plead. He was sent to Ashworth high-security hospital, where he will be held indefinitely in a psychiatric unit.

It was said that Read had attacked and killed Paul Cooper after becoming fixated with the idea he had been indecently assaulted by him when he was a child.

'Paul and Read knew each other from years earlier,' said Detective Chief Inspector McMahon. 'We have never received any allegation that Paul indecently assaulted Read at any time. There is no evidence to suggest that Paul was ever involved in any sexual offence. He had never been arrested, questioned or convicted of any crime of a sexual nature.'

Over a prolonged period of time and in a one-man vigilante campaign, Read had persuaded a number of people in the community that Cooper, and others in the area, were sex offenders.

'Many of those he spoke to believed him,' said Detective Chief Inspector McMahon, 'and this misinformation hampered our investigation in its early stages.'

Many of those targeted by such gangs are lonely misfits who fail to fit in and are incapable of defending themselves. Some, such as Paul Webster, could not take the pressure of false accusation. An inquest in Plymouth heard that the 38-year-old unemployed musician drank himself to death after neighbours accused him of being a child abuser. Webster, who had been giving children guitar lessons, was threatened with a knife and harassed constantly for three weeks by neighbours. 'Beware nonce lives here' was sprayed on the door of his flat. Relatives said the harassment continued because Webster, who had separated from his wife, was an alcoholic loner, making him an easy target for bullies. After his death, the inquest was told that the rumours of paedophilia were groundless.

Alfred Wilkins was found murdered in his home in February 2001, following a sustained period of harassment by vigilante groups. The 67-year-old former merchant seaman had been cleared of three counts of indecently assaulting a nine-year-old girl in November 2000. But this did not stop a hate campaign being focused on him and his Arundel Walk flat on the Yarborough estate in Grimsby. The terrified pensioner had made more than eighty calls for help to the police before he was murdered. His windows were smashed. People banged on his windows and doors, and 'nonce' was daubed on his home. Eight days before he was slain two intruders had broken in and punched and kicked him, leaving him with a gash to the head. The charred remains of Mr Wilkins, and his dog, Lucky, were found in the flat on 9 February 2001. The police said Mr Wilkins and Lucky had died of smoke inhalation after turpentine was poured through his letterbox and set alight. With his smashed windows boarded up, Wilkins was unable to escape and perished in the fire. After his death, the police admitted that they should have given the Grimsby pensioner more help to fend off the vigilantes.

Detective Superintendent Gavin Baggs of the Humberside Police said: 'Mr Wilkins was an elderly man with mobility problems. He lived a quiet life on the Yarborough estate. He did face a long period of harassment following his acquittal in November, and this harassment escalated to the point where he was attacked and murdered in his own home. Following the acquittal of Alfred Wilkins at Grimsby Crown court, he did face an escalating series of incidents against him and his home. Many of these were quite trivial in themselves, such as people banging on his door and windows, but I do recognise the seriousness of these incidents as they did, of course, culminate in his murder.'

He added that it had been hard to help Wilkins, as the nature of the abuse made him reluctant to speak out against those who were attacking him. However, Detective Superintendent Baggs said new procedures had been put in place to ensure no one else would suffer as Mr Wilkins had.

Sometimes, seemingly trivial matters get out of hand. Christopher Lewis, 22, and Marvin Walker, 21, frogmarched sixteen-year-old Shane Owoo to a water-filled clay pit in Bilston, West Midlands, following a dispute about a stolen bike. They forced the teenager to go for a 'punishment swim', poking him with a branch and kicking gravel at him when he tried to get out. They persisted with this harassment even when it was clear that the boy was in difficulties. Eventually, the exhausted boy drowned. His body was recovered the following day.

Lewis and Walker were jailed for five and a half years after admitting manslaughter.

'This was a long and terrifying ordeal deliberately inflicted on Shane Owoo,' said Judge Peter Coulson at Birmingham Crown court. It was 'extraordinarily callous behaviour.'

Owoo's family were devastated.

'The biggest problem we are struggling to come to terms with is knowing how he died,' said Shane's aunt Pauline Fox. 'I do not think anybody needs to go through what he went through. There was no reason whatsoever. It is something we are never going to be able to get over. To be treated in the way he was treated is really unforgivable.'

CHAPTER 12
POLICING THE POLICE

Self-appointed internet policeman John Derek Vokes, who once helped snare a paedophile, was himself jailed on 26 September 2008 for distributing child pornography with his computer. Vokes, 42, from Carrickfergus, County Antrim, claimed he was trawling the internet looking for more perverts to catch. However, he had fourteen different internet usernames and downloaded the images for his own perverted interest and sexual gratification, Antrim Crown court was told. Judge Piers Grant rejected his claims that he accessed and distributed the indecent photographs for 'benign and publicly spirited purposes'. While it was accepted he had helped the authorities in the past, the judge was satisfied he tried to use his status as 'an excuse and a protective cover' for his activities by giving the impression he was 'on the side of law and order and thereby avoid police investigation and prosecution.'

Judge Grant acknowledged that Vokes was not the

source of the images, but that in no way relieved him of his moral responsibility and that by accessing and then distributing them he was 'perpetuating the wrong'. Without people like him, child pornography on the internet would have no audience.

In 2001 Vokes had gone to police to report a man he uncovered on the internet indulging in child pornography. While the suspect was prosecuted, Vokes was warned not to surf child internet sites in future. But he did not stop. In April 2006 police seized his computer and software and uncovered a total of 230 indecent images, 132 of which 'he distributed, sent out, to those with a similar nefarious interest in child pornography,' the prosecution said.

Vokes pleaded guilty to eight specimen charges of making indecent images of a child and eight of distributing such images. He was jailed for two years and agreed to serve a further eighteen months' probation after his release. He was also banned from working with children or vulnerable adults and put on the Sex Offenders' Register for life.

Ex-policeman Geoffrey Harries, 49, was facing child pornography charges when his neighbour, 30-year-old Daniel Williams, took the law into his own hands. He stabbed Harries twenty times but claimed he was acting in self-defence. Harries confronted Williams early one Sunday morning outside his home on the Dythel Park estate in Trimsaran, near Llanelli in Carmarthen, South Wales, when he found his assailant tampering with his car. Williams had donned a black balaclava and dark hoodie, and was slashing the tyres of Mr Harries' car with a combat knife.

Harries' wife Elizabeth had alerted her husband after hearing a noise outside the house in the early hours of 7 June. She looked out of her bedroom window to see a man crouching behind a van. Her husband, who had resigned from the Dyfed-Powys police force over the child pornography charge, went to investigate. She followed. A few moments later she saw her husband facing someone in the middle of the road.

'He had his hood up and I could not see his face,' Mrs Harries said. 'Geoff was saying, "I haven't done anything. I would never do anything like that." He was saying it in a pleading tone.'

Mrs Harries shouted, 'Can't you leave us alone. He hasn't done anything to anybody.'

The man ran off and Mrs Harries saw something metallic reflected in the street light.

'My husband turned to face me and said, "I have been stabbed",' she said. 'He was stumbling and staggering. He collapsed in my arms.'

Mrs Harries tried to stem the bleeding but with little success. While they waited for the ambulance, Harries said that he recognised his attacker.

Mr Harries was taken to West Wales General Hospital,

Carmarthen, and later transferred to Morriston Hospital, Swansea, where he died of his wounds. One of the twenty stab wounds had penetrated his back and pierced his right lung.

Locals in Trimsaran said there had been hostility towards Harries since he and his wife Elizabeth moved there earlier that year. They had moved out of their old home in Pembrey, three miles away, amid similar public outrage and 'hostile incidents' after Harries was accused of possessing more than 2,082 indecent images of children on his computer. Nine of them were classed as level five category – the most serious on the scale – and fifty-two as level four. The veteran PC was charged with fifteen offences of making indecent images of children and one of possession, and was due to appear in the Cardiff Crown court on child pornography charges. A condition of his bail was that he move away from his former home in Pembrey, so he moved in with his mother in Trimsaran.

An elderly widow living nearby said: 'I know people believed that he had had problems where he was living before because of the publicity connected with his case. The gossip is that he was forced out of Pembrey and moved here. It is hard to believe that what has now happened to him isn't connected with that. This has come as a terrible shock to the village. A lot of people think he has been targeted, particularly because he was a former policeman.'

Christine Davies, another resident, agreed that the local were uneasy when Harries moved into the village.

'There was a public meeting due to take place some time this week down at the new leisure centre,' she said after the stabbing, 'and I know there was talk of a petition as well. I was talking to people when I took the bus today and some were saying "Good riddance" if he had really done what he was accused of doing.'

Local cockle-picker Adrian Jones said: 'There is a feeling in the village that he only got as good as he deserved. I have got four children myself but I wouldn't have said anything like that. Anything he has done wrong should be for the courts to decide.'

Another neighbour said: 'It is shocking. We don't know if the murder had anything to do with the forthcoming court case but it was the talk of the village. No one likes having an alleged paedophile living in your street.'

Residents had already raised a petition against Harries. Williams had obviously got wind of the controversy. Before the killing he had been out drinking for a large part of the afternoon and most of the evening. Williams claimed he had been pursued by Harries after he had been seen in the street outside his home. He said he had been attacked by the former policeman and hit out with the knife in error, claiming he had forgotten he was carrying it.

In June 2008 Swansea Crown court cleared Williams

of murder, but found him guilty of manslaughter after over a week of deliberation. Passing sentence, High Court judge Mr Justice Flaux said that the jury had dismissed Williams's version of events.

'On the night in question, you went out dressed in a balaclava, hoodie and carrying a knife,' he said. 'You set yourself up as some sort of self-proclaimed vigilante.'

Mr Justice Flaux told the court he had read a 'deeply affecting' victim impact statement written by Elizabeth Harries, the widow of the deceased. He told Williams: 'If you carry a knife on the streets, you must expect severe punishment if that knife is used to cause the death of someone.' He sentenced him to ten years.

Detective Constable Patrick Lavelle turned vigilante when he found out that a man had been bailed after attacking his son with a glass on a night out. He used the police national computer system to get the suspect's address. Visiting his house at night, he broke in and began punching a man asleep on the sofa in the face. But it was the wrong man. Liverpool Crown court heard the suspect, 22-year-old Andrew Harrop was out and Lavelle had instead battered his innocent flatmate Michael Jones, aged 23. Even though Jones protested his innocence, Lavelle did not stop hitting him until another flatmate appeared and managed to wrestle the disgraced officer off. Jones suffered concussion and extensive facial bruising.

Lavelle left the flat, but later he phoned Harrop, threatening him and insisting that he admit the attack on his son. An hour later Lavelle enlisted drinking buddy 43-year-old Stephen Keaney, of Malthouse Way, Penwortham, to phone Harrop as well.

Martin Reid, prosecuting, told Liverpool Crown court: 'Keaney told Mr Harrop, "Plead guilty, put your hands up to glassing my mate. If you don't we are coming down to sort you out. We are not fucking about and we know where you fucking live."'

The day after the attack, Lavelle, a married father of three, discovered that a complaint had been made at Preston police station. He admitted the offence and was dismissed from the police force.

His barrister Anthony O'Donohue described his client's behaviour as 'an aberration', but insisted Lavelle had already paid a heavy price for his actions.

'This is a great pity and a terrible shame Patrick Lavelle, two years from retirement and a distinguished career in the police, is being sentenced for these crimes,' he said.

Lavelle had been distressed over the attack on his son and, in an unrelated incident, his daughter was attacked and had her arm broken. These two events, particularly the assault on his son, had put Lavelle in an emotional state and caused him to behave out of character, O'Donohue said. Lavelle admitted assault and two counts of perverting the course of justice.

Sentencing, Judge Mark Brown said: 'You more than most should have realised that taking the law into your own hands is totally unacceptable. Having worked for years to make sure the ends of justice were met, you decided to wreak your own revenge. You have lost your job, suffered considerable financial loss and also brought disgrace upon yourself.'

Lavelle was jailed for twelve months. He was kept in protective custody in jail and was instructed to attend Alcoholics Anonymous.

Meanwhile Keaney, of Preston, admitted perverting the course of justice and was sentenced to sixteen weeks in jail, suspended for two years. Harrop, who permanently scarred Lavelle's son's face, was given a community order after pleading guilty to the assault.

Sixty-three-year-old Geoff Smith saw himself as part of the emergency services. In 2008, he boasted of riding his motorbike at the speed limit while using a camera mounted on his helmet to film other motorcyclists overtaking, before sending the footage to the police.

'I record all the idiots that, while I'm doing the normal correct speed, are flying past at eighty or ninety mph,' he said at the time.

Smith, from Southampton, rode a Honda Pan European, an ex-police bike which still resembled a police motorcycle thanks to livery and extra lights he had added. Despite having no powers to stop, he admitted pulling riders over and giving them a lecture at the roadside. But Smith's activities were curtailed after he had a collision with a car. He suffered cuts and bruises.

'I was knocked off by a taxi driver,' he said. 'I've done my shoulder and back. I'm still getting better. My shoulder is bruised and badly swollen.'

However, his bike, which had clocked up over 200,000 miles, was written off by insurers.

Readers of *Motorcycle News* were relieved. The paper had previously revealed Smith's own record was far from perfect. He had convictions for speeding and driving without a licence. He had also been jailed for running a crooked ambulance charity. His company, Solent Ambulance Service, was supposed to deliver human organs for transplants, but Smith had pocketed donations while living out his fantasy of being part of the emergency services by driving with lights flashing and siren sounding.

Motorcycle News reported that Smith was planning to buy the bike back from the insurers and repair it.

CHAPTER 13
FAMILY FACTORS

In 2007 a desperate mother pleaded for her paedophile son to be locked up for his own safety after their home was attacked by local people. Nineteen-year-old convicted sex offender Anthony Davies breached a Sexual Offences Prevention Order when he persuaded four children aged eleven and twelve to go on a fishing trip with him without their parents' knowledge. However, the judge refused to jail him.

Judge Francis Gilbert, QC, told Plymouth Crown court that, while Davies had breached the terms of his order by taking the children fishing, he had not actually abused them. As no contact crime had taken place, he said he could not impose a lengthy prison term, adding that it would be better for Davies to be given help rather than be sent to prison.

'Being a danger isn't an offence,' Judge Gilbert told Plymouth Crown court, 'and I have to sentence him for what he has done, not what he may do.'

Earlier in the year, Davies had been convicted of

possessing 1,200 indecent images of children and given an eighteen-month jail sentence, but he walked free because he had already served nine months on remand. He had also been charged with abducting a five-year-old boy and a ten-year-old girl in April and indecently assaulting the girl – all of which he denied. The abduction charge was dropped and the indecent assault remained on file. On his release, Davies was made the subject of a prevention order, banning contact with children. Within a month, he had taken the children fishing and faced serving the remaining nine months of his earlier sentence as well as any fresh penalty the judge imposed.

The court heard that Davies groomed young children on an internet forum he created in 2004, where he encouraged youngsters to talk about their sex lives. Several experts' reports described him as being a danger to children and said he was likely to reoffend.

Dan Norris, Labour MP for Wansdyke and a prominent child welfare campaigner, said: 'The public should be outraged and dismayed that a man with these convictions is sentenced with this upside-down thinking. The purpose of the courts is to protect the public. The judge's logic is completely outrageous – he is taking a chance and children are being put at risk. If Davies needs psychological help, he can get therapy in prison – that is part of the point of a custodial sentence.'

Neighbours in Plymouth described Davies as a

'dangerous monster who should be behind bars'. Michelle Collins, a 24-year-old mother of two who lives next door to Davies, said: 'I am horrified at the judge's comments and decision. Davies is a danger and I don't want him anywhere near my children. I don't even let them play outside if he is around.'

Some local people resorted to direct action. The windows of Davies' Plymouth home had to be boarded up after being smashed by vigilante gangs.

Convicted Jamaican paedophile Courtney Burry was granted permission to appeal against repeated deportation orders on the grounds that his human rights would be violated if he was forced to return to the West Indies – where vigilantes target criminals such as him – even though he had attracted threats from local vigilantes in Scotland where he was living. The 42-year-old child molester moved north of the border and set up home in Dumbarton, near to two primary schools. He voluntarily added his name to the Sex Offenders' Register while awaiting deportation. But for ten years he was at large in Scotland with no restrictions on his movements. Then after local vigilantes threatened to take the law into their own hands, a CCTV camera was installed to keeps his mid-terrace council home under 24-hour surveillance. The house was pelted with eggs and vandalised. The family, including Burry's 48-year-old wife Agnes, from Skye, and their two primary-age children, had to be rehoused after it was feared that attacks using petrol bombs were being planned. Burry argued that if he were deported it would violate his human rights because he would be separated from his wife and children. Agnes did not wish to move to the Caribbean because she believed that she would be victimised there because she was white and married to a child molester.

A 43-year-old woman who began a vigilante campaign against her adoptive father, a convicted paedophile, was arrested for breaching the peace. She had been delivering leaflets warning people that her father – who was jailed for seven years in 2003 on ten counts of raping and abusing her – was living on their street in Haverfordwest, Pembrokeshire, near where she lived. When the police arrived, they told her to stop or face arrest. She refused.

'I would not be told like a naughty schoolgirl to drive away,' she said. 'I had to stand up for what I believed in. I said you either let me continue what I'm doing or arrest me.'

The police obliged.

'They put me in the back of a big van with grilles on the door, took all my jewellery off me, asked me loads of questions and put me in a detention room. The police officers were brilliant, but I was the one treated like a criminal while he was being protected.'

Although she said she did not want vigilantes smashing her father's windows, 'I've got to do something... I can't believe they would just stick him under my nose like this. I went through hell all those years. I nearly killed myself over all this. It's very unfair.'

She said she had been told by the probation service she would be warned of her father's release and his new address, but it had not happened.

'I had just got back from holiday with my family on Sunday afternoon when I found out he had been living in Haverfordwest for nearly four weeks and no one had told me,' she said.

It was then that she took the law into her own hands and started her campaign.

The wife of convicted paedophile Derek Williams, who vowed to stay loyal, dumped him after neighbours on the Penygwndwn estate in Blaenau Ffestiniog led a campaign to get him kicked out of his council house and she feared vigilante reprisals. Dutch-born Ingrid met her future husband in an internet chatroom five years before and had moved from the Netherlands with him two years later. She had vowed to stand by her husband in 2007 when he walked free after being convicted of downloading child pornography. A judge freed Williams after Home Secretary John Reid pleaded for prisons to be used sparingly amid Britain's overcrowding crisis.

After Williams walked free, Dr Reid faced a barrage of criticism over the lenient sentence. There were protests from politicians, the Archbishop of Canterbury, legal authorities and charity workers. However, Williams insisted he was not the kind of paedophile who molested youngsters. And in a show of defiance, his wife posed for newspaper photographs to show how she was standing by him.

In one interview she said she had shopped her husband to the police after finding three pornographic images – of a naked girl and two teenage boys – on his computer. But she later came to believe that her husband was innocent, backing his story by saying that the images must have already been on the hard drive when they bought the computer second-hand. And when he was spared jail, the couple insisted their marriage was solid as rock.

However, he was later jailed for eight months after disobeying a court order to sign the Sex Offenders' Register within seventy-two hours of walking free from Mold Crown court. Returning to court, he also admitted being in breach of a six-month suspended prison sentence imposed earlier after he had pleaded guilty to nine counts of possessing child porn. Nevertheless, Williams still expected his wife to be waiting at the prison gates when he was freed. But five days before he was due to be released, she packed her bags and moved out of the family home. There were sightings of her in Colwyn Bay and

Llandudno, but she would not answer her mobile phone.

Eric Williams, Derek's father and a former chairman of the Penygwndwn Tenants' Association, said: 'Ingrid has left Derek and none of us can understand why. It is shocking. When Derek was in court at the beginning of the year, Ingrid agreed to stand by him. She said a lot of things. She just left one morning, taking her daughter with her. We have not been able to contact her. As far as I am concerned, the marriage is over.'

Derek Williams, a father of two, was said to be 'heart-broken'. He had lost his job and dare not return to his home for fear of vigilante action.

'Derek has still got his council house,' said his father, 'but is living in a bail hostel in Bangor now because there is still a lot of hostility in the area. He won't come back.'

And vigilantes can be dangerous. A vigilante with a petrol bomb went looking for a group who had attacked his girlfriend, the High Court in Glasgow was told in May 2009. The police said that 26-year-old Richard Scotland was seen at 1.20 a.m. standing in a street holding a bottle filled with petrol which had a cloth hanging from its neck.

'The accused was asked by officers: "What is this?"' said Prosecutor Graeme Jessop. 'And he replied: "I made it in my shed. Did you see what they did to my girl-friend's face? I'm going to do them in."'

The police had been called to Gayne Drive after a report of a disturbance there, but found only the defendant Scotland.

'During the initial disturbance that night the accused's girlfriend Katherine Devine was assaulted,' said Jessop. 'At the time of his arrest Scotland was walking in the direction of the home of her alleged assailants.'

Scotland admitted possessing an explosive device – a petrol bomb – in Gayne Drive, Glenboig, near Coatbridge, north Lanarkshire, with intent to endanger life or cause serious injury to property.

Unbeaten super-flyweight boxer 21-year-old Ashley Sexton and his 41-year-old father Lee Sexton of Eastfield Road, Waltham Cross, were charged with racially aggravated actual bodily harm and common assault after a vigilante attack on a Turkish man at Cheshunt train station on 16 April 2007 after an attempted citizen's arrest went wrong.

Sexton, then ranked number six in Great Britain, told police that Bayram Eren had been part of a gang that attacked him and his girlfriend on the same train line days earlier. After spotting men they thought were the perpetrators, they chased after them and apprehended Eren and another man. But they were the ones who ended up being charged with assault.

The incident was witnessed by Mandy Smith, former teen bride of Rolling Stones' bass guitarist Bill Wyman.

She indicated she would be unwilling to appear in court, and Eren refused to assist the prosecution. Consequently, both charges were dropped after the Sextons agreed to be bound over to keep the peace for twelve months at St Albans Crown court.

Judge Simon Carr was plainly sympathetic.

'To me, although they have cautions for violence they are clearly men of good character,' he said. 'Noting the complainant's attitude in this case there's a considerable basis of truth of why they did it. Although you felt justified to act like you did that day it amounts to vigilantism. And if people act like that the whole fabric of society falls apart. But it was two years ago and if you stay out of trouble for twelve months that's the end of it.'

The wife of 61-year-old environmental campaigner Leonard Michael Young, who was accused of groping two teenage girls in May 2009, had to run the gauntlet after their house came under attack.

'This case has received wide coverage and feelings have been running high in the neighbourhood, partly as a result of that. It's had something of an impact in the community,' defence counsel Alexander Krikler told Durham Crown court.

'Vigilantes appear to have attacked your home and that's outrageous behaviour,' said Judge Richard Lowden as he jailed Young for eight months. 'I hope the police will do their duty as your wife is in no way deserving of such an attack.'

The lover of 44-year-old Ronnie Dunbar, who was found guilty of strangling fourteen-year-old Melissa Mahon and dumping her body in the River Bonnet, Sligo, armed herself with a hatchet, hammer and acid for protection when she feared vigilantes were plotting to wipe out her young family. Twenty-five-year-old mother-of-two Ruth Nooney, who has a baby son by the child-killer, said: 'If anyone comes near my home when my kids are here I will do whatever it takes to protect them. I know what some sick people are capable of and if they come here with guns or petrol bombs I will do my utmost to defend myself. I know people are out to get me because of Ronnie.'

The Gardai were already investigating a threat made just hours after Dunbar was convicted, when a thug shouted 'You're dead' at Ruth. She said, 'I am a total outcast now and a prisoner in my own home but the only crime I committed was to fall in love.'

She had given evidence in Dunbar's defence. She vowed to stand by him despite getting death-threats from local vigilantes and being disowned by her family. But the stress of being shunned and living in fear became unbearable. Three weeks after Dunbar was convicted, Nooney dumped him. In an angry phone call to Dunbar in Castlerea Prison, County Roscommon, she told him: 'You're on your own. I can't do this any more. It's over.'

'I still love Ronnie,' she told the newspapers, 'but this case has ruined my life and my boys have to come first. I thought I could wait for him and we could have more children, but I have to devote all my time to my two babies. I am wiping my hands of this whole situation and moving to Galway. I'm down to eight stone because of all the stress.'

During his trial, the thug denied he had been having sex with Melissa and that the teenager was pregnant when she died. After his arrest, Dunbar tried to pin the crime on his eighteen-year-old daughter Samantha, who testified against her father. When Melissa's remains were recovered from Lough Gill, Samantha had told the gardai that her father had killed her friend.

Nooney hoped that her move to Galway might improve her relationship with her estranged family, but she was also fleeing Sligo because of the people there.

'I've had enough of Sligo because of all the nasty things that were said about me,' she said, 'and I just think I could have a better life for myself and the kids in Galway ... Now that I've dumped Ronnie, I hope this might allow things to get better. I have two beautiful sons, and I just hope they can get to know their family.'

*

The family of nursery worker Vanessa George found themselves in danger after she was charged with making, possessing and distributing indecent images of children in Plymouth in June 2009. Her husband Andrew, 41, who works for a catering equipment firm, and their two teenage daughters were led away from the family home under blankets. Fearful of vigilante attacks, they were taken to a safe house. The girls also had to be taken out of school.

'Her daughters went there for a day this week but were subject to the attentions of classmates,' said a friend after Vanessa George was arrested. 'They had a very rough ride. The other kids were abusive to them and tormented them. They are innocent pawns in this whole sorry mess.'

Even the Georges' neighbours in the suburb of Efford, about a mile from the Little Ted's nursery where she worked, accepted the risk of revenge attacks. One neighbour, Barbara Dean, said: 'I think there will be trouble once this gets around. They will petrol-bomb the house – that's what they're like around here.'

Her husband Martyn added: 'I dread to think what's going to happen now. This is a quiet little estate and I dread to think what kind of people might come round. I don't want any riots in my neighbourhood.'

More than a hundred parents gathered at a meeting in a church hall within hours of George's arrest to express their concern.

In a statement Mr George said: 'Myself, my two children and family have been shocked by the information and events of the past three days.' A window of the Georges' Vauxhall Astra car was smashed one night in the drive of the family home.

When Vanessa George appeared before magistrates in Plymouth on 11 June 2009, she was met with taunts and threats of violence. For her own safety, she was smuggled into the court building at 7 a.m., three hours before the hearing.

As George entered the dock, one mother shouted: 'Look at us in the face you bitch.'

Another woman in the public gallery shouted 'Oh my God' while two men fled the courtroom – one of them sobbing openly – as the charges were read out in court. Another man rushed forward to spit in her face.

Riot squads in armoured vans were placed on standby and extra court security staff were on duty as more than a hundred members of the public descended on the court building. As George was driven away in a police van with blacked-out windows, missiles were thrown at the vehicle and demonstrators broke through the police security cordon. A group of forty protesters surged forward through specially erected barriers to chase after the van as it sped away. Violence erupted when demonstrators smashed their fists against the vehicle. Two men were taken from the scene in handcuffs after being arrested on suspicion of causing criminal damage. A window of the police van was smashed during the mêlée.

The junkie mother of murdered toddler Brandon Muir was hounded out of her Dundee home by vigilantes. Twenty-three-year-old prostitute Heather Boyd was being shunted round safe houses following the horrific death of her 23-month-old son. She had been a marked woman since her lover Robert Cunningham was jailed for killing Brandon. The High Court in Glasgow heard that Cunningham hit Brandon so hard his intestines split – leaving the boy to die in agony. He was sentenced to ten years for culpable homicide.

Boyd herself was cleared of culpable homicide over claims she failed to get medical help for her child. However, many ordinary people thought she was to blame. A source close to the family said: 'She was being subjected to abuse from a couple of vigilante-style mobs who were sickened by the whole affair, and it was decided to get her out the city.'

It emerged she is being shifted from one Tayside village to another as the authorities try to find her a secure hiding-place from the hate mobs. At one time, the heroin addict was recently housed in a bedsit above a pub in the sleepy market town of Alyth, Perthshire, but she had been moved after locals got wind of who she was.

One Alyth local said: 'It might be the case that she

is moved, moved and moved again. Her face is well known and folk just don't want her around.'

Another said: 'Folk around here are good people and they certainly didn't want a known prostitute and drug user around – never mind someone who has been involved in the kind of things she has.'

Boyd herself blamed social workers for not warning her Cunningham had a violent temper.

'If I had known what Robert was like with kids I would never have gone near him,' she said.

CHAPTER 14
DRUGS BUST

Father of three Peter Drummond, 26, took the law into his own hands, claiming that his family had been 'torn apart by heroin'. On 15 February 2009, he burst into drug-dealer John Nellies' flat in Blairgowrie, Perthshire, and accused him of supplying drugs to his brother-in-law. He threatened Nellies and, finding five bags of heroin in the living room, flushed them down the lavatory. While Drummond was at Nellies' flat, drug addict Lesley Brown turned up to buy heroin. Drummond swore at her and told her to get out. She called the police and Drummond was arrested.

Justifying his actions, Drummond told the police: 'Over the last six or seven months, my family has been in hell. My brother-in-law is on smack and is getting it from the people there. It was a spur-of-the-moment thing.'

Drummond was also suitably contrite about his vigilante action.

'I shouldn't have done it but these people are ruining my family by supplying heroin,' he said. 'It is causing a family crisis and everyone is going through hell. Things have been so bad that I lost it and decided to try to stop the drug-dealing going on. I know I have done wrong. I'm sorry. I know I went about things the wrong way, but things just got on top of me.'

Drummond was held overnight and appeared in Perth sheriff court the following day. He admitted breach of the peace, but shook his head in disbelief as Sheriff Robert McCreadie jailed him for two months. Meanwhile Nellies had not even been questioned.

The court was told that Nellies was a well-known drug-dealer in the town and that he had sold heroin to the partner of Drummond's sister.

'On Sunday at 5.30 p.m., the accused, who was under the influence of alcohol, went to the address and demanded entry,' said the prosecutor. 'Mr Drummond was allowed into the hallway and began shouting and swearing at Nellies about being "a fucking drug dealer",' said the prosecutor. 'Nellies and his girlfriend are habitual drug abusers and Nellies is also known as a dealer in heroin. The accused threatened to kill Nellies if he continued to supply heroin to members of his family. He recovered five bags of heroin from the living room and flushed it down the toilet in order to prevent other persons from obtaining it.'

After sentencing Sheriff McCreadie said: 'If you were concerned about it you should contact the police, not enter a house and threaten to kill someone. You can't take matters into your own hands.'

However, there was widespread disquiet about the sentence.

'The public will have been shocked about Mr Drummond's treatment by the courts in comparison to the generally lenient approach that seems to be taken towards drug-dealers,' said Tory MSP Murdo Fraser, who represents Blairgowrie. 'This concern will undoubtedly be confounded by this revelation that, in contrast to the very swift action taken against Mr Drummond, so far no action has been taken against Mr Nellies despite the fact the court clearly accepted he was in possession of a large quantity of drugs, no doubt with intent to supply them … The public would prefer to see tougher sentences handed out to drug-dealers, rather than to people at their wits' end who take the law into their own hands.'

Labour's Shadow Justice Secretary Richard Baker, MSP, said: 'Mr Drummond has been convicted already and has received a sentence of two months for an offence which many people would see as an understandable

NIGEL CAWTHORNE

reaction to the situation he was in. If somebody is accused of drug-dealing, which is an extremely serious offence, you would think that would have priority. The fact that he has not even been interviewed, let alone charged, will leave people asking whether that sends out the right signal in terms of police priorities ... Locking someone up for destroying a dealer's illicit stash appears to go against any measure of natural justice. Drug-dealers are scum who prey on our children and more needs to be done to convict them and then lock them up. I wouldn't want to encourage anyone taking the law into their own hands but anyone can understand why Mr Drummond did what he did.'

Neil McKeganey, Professor of Drugs Misuse at the University of Glasgow, said: 'It saddens and dismays me that someone concerned about drug-dealing, who took it upon themselves to do something about it, should receive such a punishment.'

A spokesman for Tayside Police pointed out that it did not help the situation when potentially vital evidence had been flushed away. Nellies, himself, denied that he was a dealer and claimed he was the victim of mistaken identity.

'I am a heroin user,' he said. 'I've never denied that. But it wasn't me that sold drugs to this guy's family. I have never sold drugs to anyone. Peter Drummond threatened my girlfriend and flushed my own stash of drugs ... The dealers live upstairs so he came to the wrong house.'

Drummond's younger brother, 22-year-old Mark, was shocked by what he saw as a miscarriage of justice.

'I can't believe that he has been jailed for this,' he said. 'He's not the criminal here. Peter is a real family man. He loves his wife and kids and would do anything to help out his sister and brother-in-law.'

And Drummond's 27-year-old wife Lisabella supported her husband's action.

'It's beyond belief – I still can't take it in,' she said. 'Peter was sure the police wouldn't do anything about it if he told them about the dealers. He doesn't like to see his family being hurt so it was the last straw for him. Now three kids are being deprived of their dad for two months while an evil heroin dealer is still punting. Where is the justice in that?'

Explaining her husband's vigilante action she said: 'Peter is very anti-drugs and knows how it can destroy lives. His uncle died a few years ago after taking a dodgy pill.' Her husband had tried to reason with Nellies and other drug-dealers. 'He had politely asked Nellies not to sell to his brother-in-law before, but he took no notice.

'He asked the boys, pleaded and begged them to stop dealing to his sister and brother-in-law. But they carried on doing it,' she said. 'Peter was at the end of his tether and felt it was the only thing he could do to stop him supplying it.'

It was later revealed that Lisabella had been recovering from the death of a baby at the time.

'Peter has had a really tough time of it lately,' she said. 'We lost a baby in December. It came early, after five and a half months. That hit Peter really hard. He has also seen the effects heroin has on people and he couldn't bear his younger sister and her partner to go through the same thing.'

The loss of the baby had hit Lisabella even harder. Since then, her husband had become her full-time carer.

'I have no idea what I'm going to do,' she said. 'I suffer from severe depression and Peter looks after me and the kids.' Their children were all under the age of five at the time. 'We can't believe he has gone to prison for flushing a drug-dealer's supply of heroin down the toilet – he should be getting a pat on the back, not the jail. Peter has warned that drug-dealer not to supply heroin to his brother-in-law and this time he just cracked.'

Drummond's friend Thomas Brown was also stunned by the sheriff's sentence. 'Jailing him is ridiculous,' he said outside the court. 'Even the lawyer was shaking his head. Heroin is killing the community and it has been tearing Peter's family apart. He shouldn't have done what he did, but at the same time, he was only trying to help his sister. He should be getting an award for trying to do his best to clean out the drug-dealers.'

The tabloids supported Drummond, stirring up public outcry with the *Sun* drawing attention to the leniency of some of Sheriff McCreadie's previous judgments.

'In October last year he dished out just 240 hours' community service to ecstasy dealer Steven Shaw – despite him selling a dad-of-one five pills hours before he died,' said the newspaper. 'Derek Hodge, 27, collapsed at a house in Perth. Medics said they couldn't be certain what killed him, but the sentence provoked fury from Derek's mum Elsie.'

Then in June 2008, Sheriff McCreadie spared dealer Iain McLennan, nineteen, of Perth because he had nice parents and a good job. McLennan was caught with £800-worth of cocaine. He was fined just £3,000. And in August that year McCreadie freed a school youth worker who had a fling with a fifteen-year-old pupil. Perth sheriff court heard David Pullar, 30, of Perth, who worked at Harris Academy in Dundee, posed a 'medium' risk of reoffending. Even so, he got just 180 hours' community service.

The *Daily Record* also attacked Sheriff McCreadie, saying he would soon be attracting more unwelcome headlines – this time for making a female lawyer cry. At a hearing earlier in April 2009, he badgered prosecutor

Charmaine Cole over why some papers were not ready. Cole tried to explain, but Sheriff McCreadie continually interrupted her. Finally, she left the court in tears. The Crown Office launched an investigation.

Immediately he was jailed, Drummond lodged an appeal and, after ten days, he was freed on bail. Meanwhile Nellies – who had a drug-dealing conviction in 2005 – was charged with drug-dealing. However, the drug charges were suddenly dropped, though he was fined £300 after admitting trying to pass forged notes.

Two months after Drummond was jailed, Sheriff McCreadie hit the headlines again by freeing 29-year-old drug-dealer Edward Livingston, who was caught red-handed with £750-worth of cocaine and fifty-five ecstasy tablets. The police found fifteen bags of cocaine, each worth £50 on the street, and ecstasy worth £165 in his tent at the music festival T in the Park at Balado, Kinross-shire.

Livingston's solicitor, John Scullion, begged Sheriff McCreadie not to jail his client because he would lose his recruitment consultancy business if he was locked up. Scullion told Perth sheriff court: 'He has a lot to lose. And if his liberty is taken from him, the majority of that will be gone.'

Scullion added: 'He is not a daft man. He is now self-employed as a recruitment consultant, having started his own business a few months ago.' Livingston said he had bought the drugs as a 'bulk purchase' for himself and a large group of friends, and was 'repentant, remorseful and ashamed of his actions'.

Sheriff McCreadie told Livingston: 'It is disgraceful beyond measure that anyone should participate in such an evil trade.' But he added: 'I note you are a first offender. You are self-employed and in a tenancy and I take account of the loss of your business and house if you are sent to prison. You do have a lot to lose.'

He gave Livingston 240 hours of community service and fined him £600. Livingston walked from court a free man.

At the appeal court in Edinburgh on 14 May, Drummond was told that he would not have to return to jail. Although he had a record of violence, his defence advocate Andrew Brown successfully argued that Drummond's threats to kill Nellies had been taken too seriously as at the time he was drunk and angry. Instead he would be fined £150. But Sheriff McCreadie's eccentric decisions continued. On 3 June, he freed 34-year-old Martin Ramsay who admitted to stealing £170-worth of perfume from Debenhams. He had a long string of convictions – fifty in one year alone – to support his heroin habit. For eighteen years he had lived on benefits and had been taking the heroin substitute methadone since he was sixteen, despite the fact he had not given up heroin. Ramsay accepted that he was likely to go to jail for his latest offence.

'I wonder what the value of that would be at the end of the day,' said Sheriff McCreadie. 'Is it possible that he will take a tumble to himself at long, long last and deal with his opiate addiction?'

Ramsay was put on probation for twelve months and ordered to carry out eighty hours of unpaid community service.

Things took an altogether different turn when a former oil-worker who claimed he was the leader of 'an elite band of vigilantes' threatened to kneecap a prostitute. Thirty-one-year-old Graham Caie said he was trying to rid the streets of Aberdeen of heroin.

On 29 December 2007, prostitute Sharline Wright suffered an horrific ordeal after getting into Caie's car. Caie drove her from Aberdeen's Miller Street to Balnagask golf course where he attacked her with a metal bar. Caie admitted seriously assaulting Ms Wright and robbing her of her handbag and was confined to the State Hospital in Carstairs, South Lanarkshire. In the High Court in Edinburgh on 8 July 2009, defence advocate Billy Adam said it was felt Caie could be moved to a 'medium secure', though his eventual release would depend on a decision by the Scottish Ministers that he no longer poses a risk.

Advocate-depute Derek Ogg, QC, prosecuting, had

told the judge that Caie believed he was the leader of 'an elite band of vigilantes, fighting against drugs and that Ms Wright had asked to sit in his car because it was cold'. But after arriving at the golf course, Mr Ogg said, Caie changed from being 'nice and friendly' to being 'manic and violent'. He demanded that she hand over her handbag, then threw her out of the car and began kicking and punching her all over her head and body. Caie then went back to his car and brought out a metal bar.

'With both hands on it he repeatedly swung it, shouting that he was going to kneecap her,' said Mr Ogg. 'He threw away her boots, into the darkness, and then succeeded in delivering several blows with the weapon to her head and knees.'

Ms Wright tried to escape by getting into the car and locking the doors but Caie smashed a window and continued to attack her with 'extraordinary violence', Mr Ogg said. Finally he drove away with her handbag, leaving the terrified woman to walk, barefoot, to a nearby road where she begged a passing driver for help. However, she was able to give police his car's registration number because, in spite of her ordeal, she had the presence of mind to wipe mud from the number plate and memorise it.

After Caie was arrested, Mr Ogg said he tried to make an 'extraordinary justification' for what he had done. 'He seemed to genuinely believe himself to be the leader of some elite band of vigilantes dedicated to eradicating the menace of drugs from the streets.'

Caie claimed that he wanted Ms Wright's bag because he thought her phone might contain the numbers of drug-dealers.

CHAPTER 15
THE FARMER'S DEFENCE

Norfolk farmer Tony Martin found himself in trouble in 1999 when he took the law into his own hands, killing one burglar and wounding another, when they invaded his home.

Fifty-four-year-old Martin lived in an isolated semi-derelict farmhouse, nicknamed 'Bleak House', in the remote village Emneth Hungate in the Fens. The house was like something from a Grimms' fairy tale, covered in creepers and ivy. The doors were hanging off. A broken lavatory sat outside the front door. Beside it was a Rover 2000 covered in moss and a long-discarded washing machine.

Martin was considered eccentric, outspoken, solitary and highly strung – perhaps even a little loony – by friends and neighbours. He only ever wore navy-blue. Most believed him to be weird but harmless. But others, who had heard him express his hatred for burglars and what he would do with them if he caught them, had given Martin a wide berth. He also nursed a particular hatred for gypsies. He talked of putting travellers in the middle of a field surrounded with barbed wire and mowing them down with a machine gun.

Farms in Norfolk have long attracted travelling people, who come to pick the different fruits of the season. As work became less certain elsewhere, they began to settle. To Martin, they were nothing but 'light-fingered pikeys' and 'bastards'.

'He doesn't like caravan people – or gypsies and diddies as he calls them,' said Malcolm Quince, a representative of the local Neighbourhood Watch. 'There's something about him. He's never been married and I reckon he's just a strange boy. He wouldn't treat you civil if you went over there. People were just wary of him. I don't know anybody round here who was friends with him or spoke to him.'

Born in 1944 in the Cambridgeshire village of Wisbech, just a few miles from Bleak House, Martin was the son of a wealthy fruit farmer who married Hilary Mitcham, also from a farming family. He was privately educated, but proved none too bright academically. However, he won a prize for sports. A loner from an early age, Martin preferred quieter pursuits such as making models and, throughout his life, collected teddy bears.

He was also familiar with guns. They have always been part of the culture in Norfolk. Farmers use them every day. There were always guns around the Martins' house. Cartridges were kept all over the place in pots and drawers. However, his mother claimed that Tony did not take to shooting like his father and brother Robin.

'He didn't really like the idea of killing,' she said. 'He didn't like animals to be killed. When he got his own place, which is now a bit of a mess admittedly, he wanted it to be a bird sanctuary.'

After leaving school at seventeen, Martin travelled the world working on cruise liners. He worked on sheep farms in Australia and spent time in New Zealand, where he was jailed as an illegal alien. Later he worked on oil rigs in the North Sea. The death of his grandfather brought him back to the Emneth area where he ran a pig farm on his parents' property.

When he was 35, Martin inherited Bleak House from his aunt Gladys and uncle Arthur. Initially he had grand plans for the red-brick Victorian property, but due to lack of money and general apathy he let it go to rack and ruin. Instead, he bought up more of the surrounding land until he owned 350 acres along with an orchard of low trees growing apples, pears and plums.

Martin had few friends, but struck up an acquaintance with Helen Lilley, the owner of the nearby Marmion House hotel. His best friend was Terry Howard, who said that Martin had become lonely in later life.

'He would never admit to that,' he said, 'but I think

he was. He would turn up at all times, a stone would rattle at my window at 7.30 a.m. and he would say, "Are you going to let me in for a coffee?"'

Howard also said that Martin could be 'hard work' sometimes.

'I would not call him a rebel,' he said, 'but he's always been his own man. At times it could make him a pain in the arse.'

During his years at Bleak House, Martin became increasingly convinced that he was a target for burglars. He said that, not long after moving in, he had arrived home one night to catch a burglar stuffing a pillow-case with trinkets, which he dropped when Martin chased him. Over the years, he said, electrical items, tools and tractor batteries had been stolen. The year before the shooting, Martin claimed that a grandfather clock was taken. Then in May, three months before his arrest, he said crooks had broken in and stolen a table, a bureau and two chests of drawers worth over £6,000.

Martin complained about police inaction over the burglaries, but the police expressed doubts that all these incidents took place. However, the supposed thefts gave Martin the excuse to take vigilante action. He armed himself with a pump-action shotgun, for which he had no licence. In the house and the surrounding orchard, he had set up an elaborate network of lookout ladders and traps. He had even removed the stairway to hinder intruders. Upstairs, his antiques were locked away in two rooms while Martin fixed up a TV and a small lamp that burned twenty-four hours a day in another. His three Rottweilers, Otto, Bruno and Daniel, lived in the middle of this chaos.

Martin distrusted the police and began fearing for his life. He slept with his clothes and boots on and kept his shotgun primed and ready by his bedside. Despite his paranoia, he rejected all forms of assistance.

Anthony Bone, a former police officer who met him at a public meeting to discuss the introduction of a farm watch scheme, said it was clear Martin had little faith in the law.

'Tony's idea seems to be, let's stop everybody joining this, let's do it my way, to take the law into one's own hands presumably,' Bone said. 'He said that self-protection was the only way.'

On the night of 20 August 1999, two burglars – 33-year-old Brendon Fearon and sixteen-year-old Fred Barras, a gypsy – broke into Bleak House. When confronted by the gun-toting farmer, they attempted to escape through a window, but were shot by Martin. Barras was hit in the back; Fearon in the leg. Despite his injury Fearon was able to get away. He was helped by a couple who lived near the house. They got him to hospital, where he was treated. Barras died of his wounds within seconds and was later found in the grounds by a police dog. Hundreds turned out for his funeral.

'I think it was something that was waiting to happen,'

said neighbour Peter Hansard. 'If it hadn't happened now it would have happened in a year or two years' time. He was a very volatile character.'

Martin also fled the farmhouse that night. He went to his mother's house, where he hid the gun. Later, he turned up at the Marmion House hotel where he stayed for the night, courtesy of his friend Helen Lilley. Three days later, Martin was charged with the murder of Barras, and the attempted murder of Fearon. He was also charged with 'possessing a firearm with intent to endanger life' and, in the case of Fearon, 'wounding with intent to cause injury'.

Released on bail, Martin dared not return to Bleak House and went into hiding. There was reportedly a £60,000 contract on his life. After two days' freedom, he was returned to Norwich prison and later to a secret address for his own safety. His home was guarded by the police twenty-four hours a day at great expense. Martin was unapologetic. He told his friends that he thought what he did was right.

'He told me he wasn't aware he'd hit anybody,' said one friend who did not want to be identified because of the death-threats. 'He said the first shot blinded and deafened him and he just kept firing. I think he's sorry that somebody actually died, but he honestly believes that once they stepped into his house they're beyond the law anyway.'

However, Martin took a completely different line at

the committal hearing. He said that he believed 'Hitler was right' in his policies towards gypsies. (An estimated 400,000 were murdered in Nazi extermination camps during World War II.) Unfortunately there were many in the rural community who would agree with him. Indeed, the police were adamant that what Martin had done went way beyond self-defence.

'What must be very much uppermost in people's minds is the feelings and sensitivity of the family because at the end of the day we've had a young sixteen-year-old boy who has met a very premature and violent death,' said Detective Chief Inspector Martin Wright, who led the investigation.

Meanwhile, on 10 January 2000, Fearon and another member of the gang, 33-year-old Darren Bark, admitted to conspiring to burgle Martin's farm-house. Fearon was sentenced to three years in prison, and Bark to thirty months, with an additional twelve months arising from previous offences. They were experienced criminals. Between them Barras, Fearon and Bark had amassed 114 convictions by the time of the break-in at Martin's house. All three men had convictions for violence and had all served custodial sentences.

The dead boy, Barras, had been born in Wakefield, West Yorkshire and had twenty-nine convictions, including assault, six for fraud and seven for theft. He had made his first court appearance at the age of thirteen and was found guilty of two assaults, obtaining property by deception and forgery offences. At fifteen he was convicted of assaulting police, theft and being drunk and disorderly, and sentenced to two months in a young offenders' institution. Four months before he was shot, he was ordered to spend twenty-four hours at an attendance centre after being convicted of burglary and theft. The week before his death, he was arrested and charged with stealing garden furniture. He was released on bail by magistrates in Newark over police objections. The bail notice was found on his body.

The dead boy's mother Ellen Barras said: 'He was a thief but he didn't deserve this.'

She had been driven to the verge of despair by his criminal career.

'He first got into trouble at twelve for stealing some bits from a shop,' she said. 'After that he seemed in and out of trouble all the time. They were just petty crimes. But even though he kept getting into trouble I never gave up on him.'

Fearon, who was born in Newark, Nottinghamshire, had thirty-three convictions including assaults, burglary and eighteen for theft. He made his first court appearance at the age of fourteen, when he was convicted of burglary and theft and given a supervision order. At 22 he served a three-month prison sentence for a string of offences involving theft, drugs and fraud. He went to prison again at 24, then again at 27 after being convicted of wounding.

Bark, also from Newark, had fifty-two convictions at the time of the shooting, including twenty for theft and five for assault. However, the police investigation at the time concentrated on Martin. While they were searching his home, the police found a sawn-off shotgun hidden in the garage. He claimed he used it for shooting pigeons. Nevertheless, he was prosecuted for possessing another – prohibited – firearm and ammunition.

Martin had a history of firearms offences spreading back twenty years. In June 1976, he went to a friend's house in some distress, brandishing a World War I revolver. He fired a shot and a pigeon was killed. In December 1987, after an argument at his brother's house, Martin used a shotgun to smash the windows. Soon after, his brother moved abroad. Then, in 1994, he found a man scrumping apples in his orchard and shot a hole in the back of his car. As a result Martin's shotgun certificate was revoked.

After Martin's arrest many people wanted to show their support. More than three hundred people crammed in to Emneth village hall and shouted and jeered at police. They made it clear that they felt a man had a right to defend himself in his own home and complained about police response times. No sympathy was expressed for the dead Barras. The farmer received hundreds of letters of support. A defence fund was set up for Martin which received cheques for as little as a pound from outraged old women.

Martin himself showed no remorse. However, his mother said: 'He does realise a terrible thing has occurred and he is very upset about it. But let me express again, it is not his fault. They should not have been there. He was not going out to shoot anybody, was he? I think it is the most terrible thing for him because it has ruined his life. His life can never be the same again. He will never feel free. These are the people who caused this problem. They should be standing in the place he is standing in now. They are the ones who caused it.'

Interviewed by the BBC, Martin said: 'We are supposed to live in a civilised society. It's not the way I have been treated. People are not aware of what it's like in the countryside. Criminals prevail. It can't be right.'

He never mentioned Barras once.

During Martin's trial in April 2000, the jury were taken on a visit to Bleak House. Before they arrived, the police were forced to clear sackloads of rubble from the floor and cut back swathes of the dangerous hogweed plant just to make it safe. However, they left the booby traps on the landing, which were pointed out to the jurors.

Martin pleaded not guilty to murdering sixteen-year-old Fred Barras. Throughout he insisted that he was a victim of crime and was acting in self-defence. But Rosamund Horwood-Smart, QC, prosecuting, maintained that Fearon and Barras had been shot 'like rats in a trap'.

The jury were told that they had the option of returning a verdict of manslaughter rather than murder, if they thought that Martin 'did not intend to kill or cause serious bodily harm'. However, the jury of six men and six women took nine hours and thirty-six minutes to find Martin guilty of murder by a majority of ten to two. There were unsubstantiated allegations that jury members had been intimidated. As the guilty verdict was read out cries of 'yes' were heard from the public gallery.

Dressed in smart blazer and floral tie, Martin remained impassive during the proceedings and did not react to the screams of joy that came from members of the Barras family.

'I hope you die in jail,' one shouted at him.

Mr Justice Owen told Martin there was only one sentence he could pass. He was sentenced to life in prison, the mandatory sentence for murder under English law. He was sentenced to another ten years, to run concurrently, for wounding Fearon and a further twelve months for possession of an illegal firearm. However, the judge made it clear that he was not unsympathetic to Martin's plight.

'This case should serve as a dire warning to all burglars who break in to people's houses,' he said, pointing out that householders could use reasonable force to defend themselves from burglary.

'People have the right to use that reasonable force and it can have tragic results,' he said.

After the trial the Barras family said that the dead boy had been fun-loving and always happy.

'Let's remember he was just sixteen and the baby of our family,' they said. 'We are devastated by our loss. The outcome of this trial can't bring him back and our loss has torn our lives apart.'

Detective Chief Inspector Wright said he took no satisfaction from the outcome of the case.

'It has been a tragedy from start to finish,' he said. 'Burglary is without doubt one of the most despicable crimes there is, but I would stress to everybody it is up to the police to resolve it and this very tragic case where there have been no winners shows that is the case.'

The verdict sparked more argument, with pro-Martin campaigners saying it was 'monstrous' to jail a man for defending his property. Once he was incarcerated in Highpoint Prison, Suffolk, letters of support began to arrive in their thousands.

Martin began an appeal immediately. His actions were supported by chocolate heir Sir Peter Cadbury, who told the BBC's *Newsnight* programme that it was legitimate for a householder to use force against an intruder 'if the householder himself feels threatened'.

'A lot of my friends sleep with loaded guns under

their beds,' he said, 'and I don't think they can be criticised for doing that, because if they ring the police, it will be thirty-five to forty minutes before a car gets there. I have had a loaded gun by my bed for the last forty years, but in July last year, when a burglar took every piece of jewellery my wife had and my wallet and a lot else, he took the gun too.'

Cadbury added that he had now armed himself with a crossbow instead, and said he would not hesitate to use it if a burglar broke in late at night.

Charlton Heston, the Oscar-winning actor and president of America's National Rifle Association, also gave his support to Martin, and William Hague, then leader of the Conservative Party, used the Martin case to indict the criminal justice system for punishing the victims not the criminals. Martin was also seen as a hero by many vigilante groups.

In the area of Norfolk where Tony Martin lived, there was a great deal of sympathy for his predicament. David Barnard, a parish councillor at Upwell, three miles from Emneth, said: 'For many isolated farmers, calling the police is not an option. You've got to fend for yourself and hope that your security is good enough. But if it's not, then what?'

Martin's neighbour Roger Western said: 'I don't see that you can call what he did murder. He was a chap defending his own life. If I had had a gun, in a similar situation, I would have shot the intruders.'

The Martin case highlighted the problem of crime in the countryside. The National Farmers Union Mutual, which insures more than two-thirds of UK farmers, estimated that rural crime cost them well over £100 million a year in the 1990s. Vehicle theft alone cost £73 million, with more than 30,000 vehicles being stolen in rural areas in 1997. While security had been tightened in urban areas, thieves began turning their attention to the countryside. NFU Mutual figures show Norfolk as having the highest incidence of rural crime, particularly burglaries and the theft of tractors and trailers. Fear of crime was compounded by the closure of rural sub-police stations and the fall in the number of front-line officers.

Emneth, particularly, had policing difficulties because it lies on the border between Norfolk and Cambridgeshire, making it a target for the travelling criminal. Consequently, most people keep dogs, positioning their kennels right in front of their homes. Visiting journalists said that there was an air of paranoia in the village. Everyone was fearful of intruders.

'Walk around the villages of Emneth and Emneth Hungate and that fear is more than palpable,' wrote Audrey Gillan in the *Guardian*. 'Signs on lamp-posts and fences warn that "guard dogs are loose", "this is a homewatch area", that "this is private property" and that "scrap dealers are not welcome".'

Many local people, she said, kept a gun not just for

hunting but for protection. One woman told her: 'They wouldn't hesitate to use it.'

They also share Martin's antipathy towards gypsies. A number of pubs have signs outside saying 'members only' to keep the travellers out.

'They used to know their place but don't now,' said one villager. Another said: 'Like all ethnic minorities, the travelling community have a chip on their shoulder.' He added that the council 'bent over backwards for them' and gave them 'all the benefits'.

'They have always come here but in the past it was just to pick fruit and they would move on to pick Brussels sprouts somewhere else,' said one woman who refused to be named. 'But now they have settled here and there's no work and they steal lawnmowers from sheds. There were a few coloured people here but they were hounded out. The locals burgled their houses and abused them.'

NFU Mutual's Tim Price said nobody should condone vigilantism, but he understood the genuine concern of farmers and the view that the police can no longer be relied on for protection. This meant that farmers such as Tony Martin were thrown back on their own devices.

After Martin's conviction, the reaction in the local villages was mixed. Some people would not talk about the murder, but would say: 'Crime here is not as bad as it is being made out to be.'

Malcolm Quince of Neighbourhood Watch said he was horrified by Martin's actions.

'Obviously the man shouldn't have done what he did,' he said. 'If they knew him they wouldn't have gone near his house cos he's a loony. He's got funny ideas.'

But many were firmly behind the farmer. One local pensioner said: 'All Fen people would have done the same thing. Fen people are independent people. I would have blown them away myself. We all wanted him to get off because they got what they deserved. Fen people would have blasted them away.'

The verdict brought into question what amount of force was considered 'reasonable' when defending one's home and property. Leading defence lawyer Ronald Thwaites, QC, said courts look closely at the sequence of actions – and whether a defendant has acted out of revenge or vindictiveness. In other cases, things turned out very differently. An Essex man who stabbed a burglar to death was not prosecuted, while a pensioner in Derbyshire who fired a shotgun towards an intruder on his allotment was charged with wounding, but was then acquitted by a jury.

Martin's appeal was considered in October 2001 by three senior judges headed by Lord Lane. Submissions by the defence that Martin had fired in self-defence were rejected. However, his barrister told the court Martin had suffered sexual abuse as a child and 'considered himself a boy of about ten'. Throughout the trial, Martin had brought one of his teddy bears to court with him and the defence submitted evidence that Martin suffered paranoid personality disorder specifically directed at anyone intruding into his home. This submission was accepted by the Court of Appeal and his conviction was overturned on the grounds of diminished responsibility. The murder conviction was replaced by one for manslaughter carrying a five-year sentence, and his ten-year sentence for wounding Fearon was reduced to three years. These sentences were to run concurrently.

When he became eligible for parole and early release, the parole board rejected his application without stating a reason. In an interview with *The Times*, the chairman of the parole board, Sir David Hatch, described Martin as 'a very dangerous man' who may still believe his action had been right.

'Some newspapers decided very early on that Mr Martin was a victim of the criminal justice system and then ultimately of the parole board,' said Hatch. 'I don't believe that to be true. Mr Martin was a very dangerous man. He shot a sixteen-year-old boy and killed him; shot him in the back at a range of about four feet. He had a gun under his bed which he should not have had. His gun had been taken away from him because the police knew he had been using it inappropriately several times. Our job, irrespective of what the press think, is to protect the public. We said he was a dangerous man and he should stay in. I am very glad that a High Court judge, on all five counts, saw it our way.'

However, Peter Sainsbury, who has been assisting Martin's legal battle, said Mr Hatch was completely wrong.

'I am amazed he has made these comments,' said Sainsbury. 'I have never heard of such a situation before. It would seem he is simply factually wrong. All hell will break loose now. A lot of questions are going to be asked about the parole board. No one can seriously suggest that Tony Martin is a danger to the public. It was argued quite clearly in the judicial review proceedings that he could be dangerous to burglars who broke into his house – not to anyone else. And a lot of people could be classed as a danger to burglars who break into their homes. If you are in a lonely farmhouse miles from anywhere, as he was, and two burglars break in, what are you supposed to do? The vast majority of the British public supports him. We have been receiving over a hundred letters a day supporting him.'

Martin challenged the parole board's decision in the High Court. Probation officers on his case said there was an 'unacceptable risk' that he might again react with excessive force if other would-be burglars intruded on his Norfolk farm and the High Court upheld the parole board's decision.

Long-time supporter Malcolm Starr said he believed

Martin had not been paroled because he refused to apologise for his actions.

'His pride is at stake and he wasn't prepared to compromise it,' he said. 'What sort of country are we living in when you have to apologise for defending your own property? It is a shocking and lamentable ruling.'

Henry Bellingham, the MP for north west Norfolk, also rallied to Martin's defence, tabling an urgent question to then Home Secretary Jack Straw.

'I'm staggered, I'm appalled and extremely surprised because Tony Martin was a model prisoner,' said the MP. 'His behaviour was exemplary and I just can't understand for the life of me why the parole board took this decision.'

On 28 July 2003, Martin was released after serving a total of three years, the maximum period he could be held, taking into consideration good behaviour. That year, Fearon was granted £5,000 in legal aid to sue Martin for £15,000 loss of earnings due to the injury he had inflicted. He also claimed that he could no longer enjoy sex and martial arts – or even bear to see shootings on television. However, the case was thrown into doubt when photographs were published in the *Sun* suggesting that Fearon's injuries were not as serious as he had claimed. At the time Fearon was back in jail, after being convicted on drugs charges. Fearon later dropped the case when Martin agreed to drop a counter-suit.

It was later claimed that Fearon's supporters planned vigilante action of their own, putting a bounty of tens of thousands of pounds on Martin's head. Meanwhile, Martin sold his version of the story to the *Daily Mirror* for a reputed sum of £125,000. In preparation for his release, Martin said he planned to protect his home with electronic gates and install an air raid siren to raise the alarm. He was also given a special police contact to call in case of trouble.

While some people considered Martin a cold-blooded killer, others saw him as a vigilante hero. Since his release Martin has appeared on the platform with the United Kingdom Independence Party. He has also endorsed the British National Party, saying that he hoped there would be a dictator in the UK. Both parties have advocated changes in the law to stop the prosecution of people defending themselves from intruders, as well as less restrictive firearm controls. He also said that he wanted to stand for election to the House of Commons, but as a convicted felon he is prevented from doing so.

Martin's uncle was Andrew Fountaine, a founder of the National Front, the forerunner of the BNP. Martin was a regular visitor to Fountaine's home, at Narford Hall, near Swaffham, Norfolk, not far from Bleak House. It was there that the National Front leader organised regular Aryan summer camps, which prompted the Home Office on one occasion to refuse entry to a number of continental fascists. Fountaine had also warned of the influx of travellers.

'Within a generation, the Norfolkman, his culture, purpose, and ethnic succession will be biologically extinguished,' he said.

By killing a gypsy, it seems that Martin had taken this message to heart.

CHAPTER 16
HOME SECURITY

An Englishman's home is his castle and some believe that he should use any means at his disposal to defend it. However, 68-year-old Len Fountain managed to shoot himself with the shotgun he had set up in his garden shed to ward off burglars. The outhouse had been broken into several times, so he rigged up a booby trap. It consisted of a home-made shotgun that used a mixture of chlorate and sulphur to fire a pellet made of newspaper from its muzzle. The weapon was slung from the ceiling of the tool shed, connected to a battery-powered electrical tripwire and aligned to fire its pellet at anyone entering.

It had been set up for about a year when, on 27 September 2000, Fountain, a self-employed agricultural contractor from Boylestone, Derbyshire, was in a hurry to do a job for a farmer and simply forgot the booby trap was there. He absent-mindedly walked into the shed without unhitching the tripwire and triggered the device, shooting himself in the leg. His 63-year-old wife

Mabel found him lying outside the shed with a serious leg injury and called for help. Paramedics who came to his cottage found him sitting on the ground beside his porch with serious injuries to his right knee and thigh. Fountain was taken to Burton hospital where his injuries were discovered to be not life-threatening. He was in hospital for two weeks.

'A search of an outbuilding used to store tools revealed a crude home-made device comprising a barrel and wire connected to the shed door,' said Detective Sergeant Steve Wain of the Derbyshire Police. 'Mr Fountain had been the victim of a burglary in the past. We believe the premises were attacked about a year ago – the same shed was broken into. This is not a particularly high crime area but this is an isolated spot.'

The bomb squad from Chilwell, Nottinghamshire, was called to make the device safe and to check the grounds to see if there were any further booby traps. In a search of the premises, the police found twelve firearms – eleven shotguns and a rifle – which they confiscated.

Inspector Glen Wicks said that the device that had injured Fountain was like a mortar filled with home-made explosives and was designed to fire straight at anyone who opened the door.

'Unfortunately, he seems to have forgotten that he set this thing up and it went off, nearly taking his leg off,' he said. 'It was an intricate design with batteries and electrical connections. Obviously, as soon as he is out of surgery and able to, we will be talking to him about this incident.'

As a result of those interviews, they charged him with possessing illegal firearms. When the case came to court, the judge ruled that Fountain should be cleared of possessing a firearm with intent to endanger life because there was no evidence he meant to harm anyone.

'I rigged up the gun to make a loud bang to frighten burglars and wake me up,' Fountain maintained.

Fountain complained that he had set up the booby trap in his shed following a spate of break-ins in the village where he had lived for forty-six years. He said burglars had taken power tools, including a new chainsaw, from his shed about a year before.

'My daughter was burgled seven times,' said Len. 'But after I got done it was the final straw. You're so angry, it obsesses you. It stews in your mind – "how can I get back at them? What can I do to stop it?" You can't settle for wanting revenge, you have to do something.'

He admitted six offences of possessing firearms without certificates and one of possessing unlawful ammunition. He was given a suspended eighteen-month jail term and fined £2,500.

Some people go to even greater lengths to protect their property. The headquarters of Joe Weston-Webb's portable flooring business at Redhill Marina near Ratcliffe-on-Soar, Nottinghamshire was ringed by a security fence with motion-sensor lights and CCTV cameras. But none of these hi-tech security measures deterred arsonists and vandals. So, in desperation, the 70-year-old ex-entertainer fortified his defences with less orthodox technology left over from his time as a travelling show-man. As part of the show he used to use a Roman ballista – a thirty-foot catapult that has now been brought out of retirement.

'We're under siege here,' he said, 'so a catapult seems like a suitable solution.'

Every evening he loaded his 'dungslinger' with chicken droppings that came from his farm nearby.

'I've got chickens so there's plenty of that and I've got some "smart water" and I'm going to mix the two together and make the bag of stuff heavier,' he said. 'The heavier it is, the further it will fly and I hope that it will hit somebody running away on the back of the neck.'

Also in his arsenal was a twenty-foot human cannon that would fire a railway sleeper if triggered by an intruder. These fearsome devices had once been used to shoot his wife across the River Avon.

Miscreants were warned about the array of armoury they faced. Outside Weston-Webb's premises, there was a sign that read: 'Warning: These premises are protected by Smart Poo and railway sleeper projectiles.'

His warehouse stood at the end of a farm track in

the lower valley of the River Soar – a place known locally as Soar Bottom.

'I have an exploding coffin too,' he said. 'The intruder would have to climb into the box in order to be blown out of it and I don't expect anyone would be stupid enough to do that, but I'm working on it.'

Weston-Webb believed that his company, Grumpy Joe's Flooring, had been a target by rivals in the portable flooring industry after he won a lucrative contract to supply the BBC show *Strictly Come Dancing*. In the early hours of 2 February 2008 arsonists started a fire that caused £2,000-worth of damage while he was asleep in his home nearby. That same night, four cars outside his daughter's house in Sileby, Leicestershire, had their tyres slashed and windows smashed.

'My daughter lives twelve miles away,' he said. 'It's too much of a coincidence. We are pretty certain it was a rival company, but I can't prove it.'

He said he had not built up his flooring business to let his rivals walk all over him. His weapons had been gathering dust and his wife's show-business days were behind her.

'She's 54 now and far too big to fit into the cannon in any case,' he said.

Mrs Weston-Webb had been one of her husband's all-girl squad of 'Motobirds'. Together, they travelled the world jumping motorcycles and cars over ramps, rivers and aquatic obstacles. After she had broken an arm and could not ride, she began her career as a human cannon-ball. Then, before an expectant crowd of 30,000, she climbed into the catapult her husband would later employ to defend his warehouses.

'I flew across 160 feet of the Avon,' she said. 'Unfortunately the net was set at an angle and I bounced into the river.'

Later Weston-Webb attempted to build a car with wings that would fly from the edge of a quarry, with disastrous results. Then there was a ramp that would allow a double-decker bus to jump the Avon. When he put his show-biz career behind him and went into the flooring business, he held on to his carny equipment, never realising that it might come in useful.

His wife stood by his decision to use their old carny equipment as booby traps. 'We just feel so helpless,' she said.

Nottinghamshire Police sent an officer to give them advice on conventional security techniques and advise them on the use of 'reasonable force'. But Weston-Webb believed that he had taken reasonable precautions.

'We are putting a rubber block on the end of the rail-way sleeper,' he said. 'It should just knock an intruder down ... That's the only concession I'm willing to make to all the do-gooders who seem to think criminals should be able to do what they want. I'm not out to kill anyone or even hurt them – I just want to keep yobs off my land. So I'm prepared to make my missiles a bit softer – but that's it.'

However, the police warned Weston-Webb that he would be prosecuted if he unleashed Britain's biggest anti-burglary device on any criminal trespassing on his property. He was warned that, if he fired his 'dungslinger', which is mounted on an old truck, it would be classified as a firearm and then it would be confiscated and he would be arrested.

'We discussed how they were going to confiscate this wrecked truck,' he said, 'and they went away scratching their heads, but they mean business.'

Nevertheless, Weston-Webb vowed to ignore the warning, saying his battle highlighted the plight of besieged home-owners across the country.

'The police seem to be hoping I'm just having a bit of a laugh at their expense,' he said. 'But they're the ones who have lost all sense of reality. This is a serious issue. People all over Britain are sick and tired of feeling like prisoners in their own homes and seeing yobs get away with it.'

Vigilante action was the only remedy.

'It's absolutely typical of this country that the person whose life has been made a complete misery is the one most likely to end up in court,' he said. 'Maybe the police think I'm joking, but the only people laughing are the criminals. That's why I fully intend to take the law into my own hands.'

Weston-Webb intended to set up a website urging other home-owners to protect their property. He said he had won huge public support.

'I've had hundreds of calls from people backing me,' he said. 'In fact, the only people who seem to be against what I'm doing are the police.'

He took action out of pure frustration.

'Everything in this country is stacked against decent, law-abiding citizens,' he told the *Daily Mail*. 'The bottom line is that you either make a stand or live in misery.'

The police were equally adamant. Inspector Jeff Haywood said: 'The law allows home-owners to protect themselves and their property with reasonable force if they are under threat from an intruder. However, the reasonable force must be proportionate to the threat. The setting up of booby traps is something that we would advise against.'

However, Harrow-educated Weston-Webb did heed the police warnings, briefly. On 13 April 2009 his ballista was not loaded and his cannon unprimed. At 11.15 p.m. his CCTV cameras picked up a shadowy figure entering his premises before going blank. Then the intruders did thousands of pounds' worth of damage.

'I blame the police for this,' he said. 'They stopped me from guarding my property – and this is the direct result. What kind of a society are we living in when the so-called forces of law and order basically invite criminals to do what they want?'

The intruders trashed machinery, rifled through filing cabinets, damaged vehicles and tried to destroy surveillance equipment.

'I could have seen these people off with the catapult. Instead I'm told I'm the one who will end up in court – and the crooks get a free hand.'

He planned to reactivate the catapult in the face of what he believes is a vendetta.

'It is ridiculous that we are in this situation now in which we can't defend ourselves,' he said. 'They warned me off, and the result is that my business has been smashed to bits by yobs.'

Although he had been told that vigilante action is against the law, he felt he had no option but to rearm his arsenal.

'I've got to do something because the police don't seem interested,' he said. 'This latest break-in happened last Monday night, but the police didn't manage to take fingerprints until Thursday morning. What am I meant to do? These people have vandalised my workshop, stolen money and machines. It will cost me £10,000 to replace them. On Monday night the burglars managed to de-activate the CCTV cameras, which the police had told me was all the security I needed. I have to do something to keep these yobs off my land.'

When he was interviewed on local radio to discuss

his plight, the station was inundated with messages of support. Many callers expressed their outrage that the police seemed more interested in arresting him rather than catching those responsible for the break-ins.

'There are still a lot of good people in this country,' said one caller, 'but the way everything works is just a complete joke. Everything in this country is stacked against decent, law-abiding citizens. The bottom line is that you either make a stand – or live in misery.'

That listener was speaking for many people who believe that they are not protected by the police and feel it necessary to take some form of vigilante action. One of them was Sean Preson, the 41-year-old boss of a building firm who took the law into his own hands. One night in August 2008, the married father of three was driving home from a restaurant with his family and saw four men breaking into his bungalow he was renovating in Huncote, Leicestershire. The burglars were trying to steal a floodlight and CCTV equipment from the site. Over the previous six months, the bungalow had been raided repeatedly and goods worth £4,500 had been stolen. Preson stopped the car and confronted one of the men, who threatened him with a screwdriver. Preson disarmed him, but the man made off in a car. Two other gang members hid, while the fourth made his escape on foot.

Preson took his family home and called 999. According to Preson, he was told: 'We'll be round in the next couple of days.'

So Preson told the operator that he would deal with the situation himself. He called 25-year-old Ashley Shepherd, an employee and friend. They decided to make a citizen's arrest. That night they tracked down one of the gang, eighteen-year-old Joshua Clarke, who was still making his getaway on foot. Shepherd knocked him down while Preson stood by with a crowbar. They forced Clarke into the back of a van and drove him back to the bungalow where they questioned him. They sprayed him with window-cleaning fluid and demanded that he take them to the ringleader's home. There they found 29-year-old Nathan Barnes – a 'big skinhead bloke' – cowering and dragged him outside in a head-lock.

'We barely touched him, but he started crying like a baby,' Preson said.

Clarke was then bundled into the back of a car and driven home. He had suffered minor injuries. Preson kept his mobile phone and keys as security against the estimated £300-worth of damage he was accused of caus-ing.

The following day the police arrested the two vigi-lantes. Preson was held in a cell for a day and a half and charged with kidnap, an offence that carries a maxi-mum sentence of life in prison. He admitted the charge, but walked free from Leicester Crown court after his defence counsel gave the judge forty references and testimonials of support. Preson was given a twelve-month sentence suspended for two years and two hundred hours of unpaid community work. Shepherd admitted assault and also received a suspended sentence and community service order for 150 hours of unpaid work.

Explaining the leniency of his sentence, Judge Michael Pert, QC said: 'I'm prepared to treat your case as an exception. I accept you were driven to distraction by people constantly burgling your premises. The fact you called the police and were told they'd send someone to see you in two days would give anybody pause for thought. Anyone would be sympathetic to the position you found yourself in.'

However, he added: 'I cannot accept what you did was right but your conduct does not warrant you being sent to prison.'

After the hearing, Preson said: 'I'm a law-abiding person. We were the victims who now come away as criminals while the culprits get off scot-free.'

The thieves, Clarke and Barnes, only received a caution. A 28-year-old woman was also cautioned, and a 24-year-old man was charged with attempted theft and given a twelve-month conditional discharge. Preson was peeved that they got off so lightly.

'We were effecting a citizen's arrest and it's ended up putting us through seven months of hell,' he said. 'We only detained the youth for about an hour, whereas I was put in a cell for thirty-six hours. I understand the lad was in fear, but I believe if someone goes on your property without your permission they should be prepared for what may happen to them. I acted out of frustration ... It's the vigilante aspect they didn't like, but all I was trying to do was to protect my property.'

Shepherd was also put out that the full force of the law had come down on them for protecting private property.

'It shouldn't have gone this far,' he said.

A spokesman for Leicestershire Police said Preson misinterpreted their response. In Leicester Crown court, Preson had said that when he rang the police he was asked: 'What's your availability in the next couple of days?'

But that was not the full extent of the conversation, the police maintained.

'We have reviewed the recording of this call and while the defendant was asked what his availability was over the next two days, he was clearly told the incident was prioritised for officers to attend that night,' the police spokesman said. 'We have to prioritise calls. It was established during the call that these intruders had left the scene twenty minutes prior to the call being made and there was no immediate risk of harm ... Officers were assigned to deal with the incident fifty minutes after the call was received. But they were diverted to deal with reports of an assault, which we later established related to offences the two defendants admitted to.'

'I'm glad it's over and the judge sympathised,' said Preson after his release. 'On reflection, I don't think I'd handle it quite the same way again. It's ironic that I'll end up doing unpaid work alongside the kind of criminals I was trying to apprehend. If the police had done their job properly, none of this would have happened.'

This is a common complaint.

Fifty-two-year-old David Bowen said he 'snapped' after a gang of youths targeted his home. They had been throwing stones and food at his house for several days. When he heard the yobs outside once more, he grabbed his twelve-bore shotgun and fired it at the gang. One of the youths was hit in the face by a pellet.

Prosecutor David Elias told Cardiff Crown court that about twenty youths aged between twelve and sixteen were outside Bowen's house in Waun Llwyd, Nantymoel, Bridgend, that night in December 2009. But they weren't causing any trouble and Bowen simply overreacted.

'When he heard the youths outside he picked up his gun and took four cartridges, loading one of them into the shotgun,' Elias said. 'Bowen swung the gun in an upwards motion and the gun went off and a shot was fired. He said he never intended to cause injury to anyone but did accept he fired the gun.'

Cardiff Crown court was told pellets struck student sixteen-year-old Ashley Coid in the shoulder and face.

'He felt it on the back of his shoulder but he was wearing three layers of clothing. He also felt it graze his right cheek,' Elias said. 'Ashley went back to confront Bowen to ask him why he'd shot at him. Bowen held the gun up and threatened to shoot him again.'

The court was told that Bowen shouted: 'Come on, come on. I've got you now. Come a bit closer.'

Two patrolling Police Community Support officers, Gareth Evans and Richard Thomas, saw the confrontation and were able to get the injured youth away from the scene. Armed response units were called, but Bowen immediately put down his weapon voluntarily.

'There have been terrible problems with youths in the area and this man snapped,' said defence counsel Hugh Wallis. 'It is Bowen who is in the dock and not those who have made his life and his neighbours' lives misery.'

Bowen, who had moved to Heol Dewi Sant, Bettws, near Bridgend, pleaded guilty to possession of a firearm with intent, common assault and failure to comply with the provision of a shotgun certificate.

Judge Michael Burr said: 'It was no great surprise that when you shot the gun at these boys one was hit and injured. That was inexcusable. This sort of response cannot be tolerated. This was a loaded gun fired with a view to frighten, instead of injuring anybody.'

He jailed Bowen for twelve months.

His partner, 43-year-old mother-of-two Sharon Morgan, of Nantymoel, Bridgend, said that the family had suffered a two and a half year torrent of abuse from youths, that had pushed her normally mild-mannered husband too far. He was, she said, a 'gentle and loving man' who had been pushed to his limit by yobs who threw 'stones, muck and food'. Her family was regularly subjected to name-calling, swearing and threats when they left the house. Her fourteen-year-old son Daniel had been bullied and threatened with violence.

'I feel like a prisoner in my own home. Daniel hasn't been to school for six weeks because he's scared,' she told *Wales on Sunday* after Bowen had been jailed. 'David wouldn't hurt a fly. I feel it's wrong that he's ended up in jail for trying to protect his own family.'

She again asserted that Bowen had never meant to hurt anyone. The shot he had fired was just intended to frighten the gang of youths away.

'He had had enough,' she said. 'For a man who's working six days a week, he just wanted to come home and have peace and quiet and watch the telly like normal men do when they've had a hard day's work. David's a calm man and doesn't have a temper. He didn't need to have these kids constantly throwing stones at the house and calling names. They just pushed him too far.'

At the time Morgan had been hanging clothes out to dry and was not aware of what was going on in the street.

'All I know is that kids were throwing stones at the window,' she said. 'The next moment I had a phone call and there was a load of armed officers outside the house pointing guns. I was shocked, I didn't know what was going on. I was crying and Daniel was crying. David has been punished, but what about the youths – why aren't they being punished?'

Other residents in the area have lent their support, saying the police had done nothing to protect them from the intimidating gangs of youths that roamed the streets.

One neighbour, 45-year-old mother-of-three Maria Gardner, said she sympathised with Bowen – her family was victimised by youths for three years.

'When I heard about what had happened I wanted to support him,' she said. 'I didn't blame him, because I know what he's been going through. I had every sympathy with him. After what we went through, I always said it was only a matter of time before something like this happened. There is only so much a person can take.'

The youths were targeting other people in Nantymoel and she was afraid that they would not have the courage to stand up to them.

'It's about time the people in this valley started sticking together,' she said. 'He shouldn't have done what he did. But knowing the way we felt when it was happening to us, if we had a gun in the house, I can't say for definite that I wouldn't have been pushed to that limit. At the end of the day he was an innocent person in his own home being terrorised – and he's the one who's gone to prison.'

Inspector Steve Evans, of Maesteg Police, rejected the claim that his officers were not taking the complaints made by locals seriously. He said that a number of anti-social behaviour referrals had been made against local youths. However, ASBOs do not stop ordinary citizens feeling that they had to take the law into their own hands, especially when they see the streets filled with gangs of feral youths.

A case in point is that of 28-year-old vigilante Jon Rutherford who jumped into his Vauxhall Vectra in just his pyjama bottoms. It was 1 a.m. and his wife had just told him that two drunken youths had kicked his car, which was parked outside their home, breaking the wing mirror. The hot-headed father of two chased the two youths around the corner. Mounting the pavement, he knocked down one of the teenagers, breaking his foot. Rutherford, a former army boxer, then jumped out of his car and punched the unconscious seventeen-year-old in the face up to eight times, yelling 'you deserve it, you deserve to die.' An eyewitness said: 'The delivery of each blow was extremely hard and vicious.'

Rutherford then took a mobile phone from the bystander to stop them calling for the police and drove back home. By then, the car had a damaged front nearside wing where it had hit a wall after striking the teenager. However, Rutherford later returned to the scene and gave the phone back to the onlooker. He was arrested shortly afterwards. The police booked him for driving under the influence of alcohol. The victim, who had no criminal record and had not been in trouble before, had five broken toes and spent sixteen days in hospital.

'The incident has had a massive negative impact on my life,' he said. 'I am not sure how long it will take to recover physically and mentally.'

Rutherford pleaded guilty to causing grievous bodily harm with intent, dangerous driving and driving with excess alcohol. Three years earlier, he had been given a suspended twelve-month jail sentence for stabbing a man twice in a street argument, Teesside Crown court was told. He boxed for two years during six years' service with the Royal Signals Corps.

Defence counsel Ian Bradshaw said that Rutherford, a labourer of Gloucester Street, Hartlepool, was 'Mr Average'.

'He told me that on both occasions he considered it to be the right and honourable thing to do that led him before the courts,' he said. 'Rutherford felt he did what anyone would do by chasing the vandal but accepted he then went completely over the top.'

Bradshaw added: 'He was ready for bed and this is a set of circumstances that is thrust upon him, but which he hopelessly and horribly misjudged.'

Rutherford later told a probation officer he only did what anybody would have done in the circumstances. The judge, Recorder Martin Bethel, told Rutherford: 'That you seek to justify your behaviour to a probation officer is frightening.'

Assessed as a high risk of being a serious danger to the public, Rutherford was jailed for three years. He was also disqualified from driving for two years.

Recorder Bethel said: 'Anybody would be angry, that at least is understandable. But you overreacted in a quite grotesque way.'

In a similar case, Judge Richard Bray criticised the police for the growing number of this type of reprisal crime that were being committed. He said that the courts ended up dealing with revenge attacks because officers did not respond to calls quickly enough. Judge Bray made these comments when he was sentencing a father and his two sons for attacking a man they thought had caused criminal damage to their car.

'Nobody bothers to phone the police any more,' said Judge Bray. 'They go round and sort it out themselves

– and I know why. It is because the police do not actually come round so people go out themselves and deal with it. Then I have to sort it out in the courts for them.'

The vigilante attack which sparked his outburst occurred on 27 July 2008 when 48-year-old Henry Smith of Bridge Road, Kettering, and his sons Ian, 23, and Jamie, 19, went round to the victim's house in Alexandra Road, Desborough, after their car had been damaged two days earlier.

Ian Smith punched the victim to the ground then he and Jamie punched and kicked him, leaving him with injuries to his face, teeth and gums. Both admitted grievous bodily harm at an earlier hearing. Ian Smith was given a fifty-week jail sentence, suspended, and ordered to pay £1,000 compensation to his victim. Jamie Smith was given a forty-week suspended sentence and ordered to pay £500 compensation. Henry Smith, who pleaded guilty to affray, was ordered to pay costs. Between them, the three were ordered to complete a total of 390 hours of unpaid community work.

Reacting to the judge's comments, a police spokesman said: 'The initial offence of criminal damage was not reported to us so we were not in a position to respond. We would always encourage people to report these offences to us rather than take matters into their own hands.'

*

Vigilante attacker Francis Hylton, who viciously assaulted with a pair of pliers the person he thought had burgled his house, was jailed for two years on 31 May 2009. During a trial at Teesside Crown court, Hylton and his friend, Michael Burke, were accused of kidnapping Jason Parker at knifepoint and disfiguring him in a terrible 25-minute attack. A jury cleared Burke, 33, of all charges, while 44-year-old Hylton of Eddison Way, Hemlington, was acquitted of kidnap and robbery. However, he pleaded guilty to assault causing actual bodily harm and stealing Parker's bicycle.

Hylton had confronted Parker in Coulby Newham on 16 November 2008 in an attempt to retrieve his new £1,000 plasma television, after he had been told that Parker was responsible for burgling his home four days earlier. He had a pair of pliers in his coat pocket and used them to cut Parker's face, nose, mouth and neck. Parker said Hylton grabbed his nose and twisted it to the extent that he needed plastic surgery. He said he also feared his drug-addled assailant would try to pull out his teeth.

Admitting assaulting Parker, Hylton said he 'laid into him ... and hit him as hard and fast as I could.' Parker was described as a six foot four inch 'bully'.

When Parker appeared in court earlier in March, he suffered another vigilante assault. He was attacked in the public gallery. This led to a lockdown of the court building. The man who threw the punch was given a six-month prison sentence.

Jonathan Walker, defending Hylton at the sentencing, told the court that the lack of remorse or empathy shown by Hylton in an interview with probation service officials was 'not surprising'.

'The offences were the culmination of a number of days of unedifying behaviour on behalf of a number of individuals,' Walker said. 'His property had been burgled. The defendant concedes that, with good sense, he should have reported it to the police and let the matter take its course.'

For Judge Peter Armstrong, it was too late for such reflection.

'You believed your house had been burgled and you took it upon yourself to deal with it, rather than go to the police,' he said. 'You had a pair of pliers, you hit him with them. He thought you were going to try to take his teeth out. He got injuries to his mouth and nose by you using those pliers.'

The use of such extreme violence demanded a jail sentence.

'This was an assault, causing unpleasant injuries by the use of a weapon, so I think it is appropriate to pass a sentence of two years,' said Judge Armstrong. 'It had the element of vigilantism about it. You must not take the law into your own hands in future because it's you who ends up getting a custodial sentence, not the other person.'

Hylton was also sentenced for possessing an offensive

weapon and being drunk and disorderly on another occasion – charges he admitted. The court was told that he was involved in a drunken row outside a property on St Barnabas Road, Linthorpe, Middlesbrough, at 3.40 a.m. on 7 October 2008. He had been out on bail when he attacked Parker. Police arrived at St Barnabas Road to find Hylton swearing, shouting 'wife-beater' and kicking the door of the house. After being asked to leave the scene, Hylton continued the abuse and made a two-fingered gesture to passing motorists before he was arrested, said Sam Andrews, prosecuting. At the police station, officers found he had a six-inch-long martial arts weapon known as a 'cubiton' on a shoelace around his neck. Hylton claimed it was a key ring.

Another self-confessed vigilante who went too far was 65-year-old pensioner Colin Coulson of Burgate, Pickering, North Yorkshire who was sentenced to thirty-six weeks' imprisonment, suspended for eighteen months at York Crown court after stabbing a sixteen-year-old stranger in the face. Coulson had been plagued by local youths for some time. On the night in question he was woken up by someone knocking on his bedroom window after climbing up scaffolding outside his home. He snapped. Grabbing a large kitchen knife he set out to find the culprit. His young victim was standing outside a takeaway shop, close to Coulson's home, waiting for a friend when the defendant walked up and, without warning, stabbed him in the cheek. The injured teenager phoned his father. Together they scoured the area. They found Coulson who produced the knife from his sleeve and started waving it at the boy's father, but he managed to disarm him and kick the knife away. Coulson was tagged for four months and ordered to pay his victim £500 compensation.

The *Plymouth Evening Herald* dubbed 62-year-old Tom Paterson the 'vigilante grandad' after he resorted to standing guard outside his house at night armed with a pickaxe handle to fight off local yobs. The residents of Crease Lane in the quiet Devon town of Tavistock had long complained that the police had done nothing to curb the gang of vandals who had plagued their neighbourhood for more than a year.

Many of the residents of Crease Lane were elderly and frail. They were being terrorised by a group of around five yobs, some as young as ten, who battered parked cars, hurled objects through windows, and urinated and even defecated on communal benches and driveways. One elderly lady was too frightened even to look out of the window at night for fear she might be seen by the gang, who once pelted her house with eggs. A neighbour's property had been sprayed with graffiti, gardens had been wrecked and road signs dented.

Finally, Paterson, a retired engineer, decided that he

would do something about it. When darkness fell, he manned his driveway with his trusty pickaxe handle in hand. Often he stayed on post until 3 a.m., ready to confront the hooligans.

'I've had enough now. I'm fed up,' he said. 'They leave a trail of destruction behind them at weekends and a lot of people have suffered. So now I go outside at about 9.30 or 10 p.m. and basically stand in front of the property and wait with a pickaxe handle. I walk up and down the garden and up and down the drive; it does get cold late at night.'

Paterson said that the youths drank or took drugs, then ran riot until the early hours. Empty vodka bottles and beer cans littered a nearby path.

'If you confront them you get a lot of verbal abuse,' he said, 'then they come back under the cover of darkness to cause more problems.'

He admitted that he was frightened that any confrontation might end in violence and he accepted that he was laying his safety on the line. But he was prepared to risk facing any reprisals to defend his property.

'It's only me and my wife here and you do feel vulnerable,' he said. 'If you get five of them against you then you could get hurt.'

As a precaution, his wife was stationed next to the telephone indoors, ready to call the police if there was any sort of altercation.

Before picking up the pickaxe handle, the Patersons had spent some £2,000 defending their home. They had installed floodlights and night-vision CCTV, but nothing seemed to deter the vandals. They had also submitted a formal complaint to Devon and Cornwall Constabulary, claiming officers rarely visited the area. When Paterson's vigilante action caught the attention of the local newspaper, the neighbourhood beat manager for Tavistock Town, PC Simon Raeburn, said the problem lay with people failing to report the trouble to police.

'Mr Paterson has highlighted a problem in the Crease Lane area which, until he did, we were unaware of,' he said. 'Unless we get an indication of what is going on we don't know where to put our troops. If this anti-social behaviour is a concern for the residents of Crease Lane then it is a concern for us. Every town has got a handful of idiots and the same handful of idiots take up a large proportion of police time.'

Mother of two Samantha Nicholson, 31, took the law into her own hands when she slapped three teenagers after her family home was terrorised by yobs. She had only moved into the council house on Lund Lane, Lundwood, Barnsley with her partner and her two children, aged ten and twelve, a week before the incident. The family had moved to the area from Grimsby so that Nicholson could look after her boyfriend's mother who is blind and disabled.

On their first day in the house a youth knocked on the door and told her: 'If your face doesn't fit you can't live here, we do, we decide and you're not living here.'

That night, taxis, takeaway pizzas and Indian meals that the family had not ordered were delivered. The wheelie bin outside the house was set on fire twice. The garden was vandalised. A gang of some thirty youths who congregated on nearby waste ground hurled stones, bricks, bottles and abuse. They played loud music from a ghetto blaster until 1 a.m. and threatened to burgle the house and burn it down. The teenagers even ran naked up and down the street to provoke the family. Nicholson, who suffers from osteoarthritis of the spine, called the police and the council, but received no help. The teenagers' reign of terror continued.

'They were throwing bricks at the windows for six hours and making threats until 11.45 one evening,' she said. 'I told them to pack it in but when they started mouthing off at me again the next day I just lost my rag.'

At around 5.45 p.m. on 23 August 2006 she tried to remonstrate with a sixteen-year-old boy and two fourteen-year-old girls after bricks had again been thrown at her windows. She was met, she said, with a 'defiant attitude'.

'You can't touch us,' they said. 'What can you do about it?'

'You think I'm all mouth,' said Nicholson, before slapping each one of them on the face.

Afterwards she told cops: 'I just did it to shock them.'

She admitted assaulting the youths at Barnsley magistrates' court.

'I only pleaded guilty in court to get it over and done with,' she said. 'I've not been too well lately and this has made it worse.'

In mitigation, Gus Kennedy said: 'She sincerely regrets she lost her temper; she was simply at the end of her tether.'

Sentencing, District Judge Rosenberg said: 'I do accept you lost your temper and I do accept there is genuine remorse. Any right-thinking person would have enormous sympathy for you. It stands out like a sore thumb that you have suffered horrendous intimidation from local youths. But you took the law into your own hands and at the end of the day you are to be dealt with for taking the law into your own hands.'

He gave Nicholson an eighteen-month community order and told her to pay £43 costs. But he did not award compensation to the three children because of the 'overall picture' of the case. Nicholson's family had been driven from the estate.

Judge Rosenberg added: 'I can't comment as to what the police have or have not done. I can't comment as to what the council has or has not done. But I'm certain any right-thinking member of society would be appalled by this. If the police and council could be asked to look at this afresh and to ensure while this lady is moving and, when she moves, some sort of assistance can be given I'd be grateful.'

Her boyfriend, 43-year-old lorry driver Anthony Kirk, said: 'It's pathetic that Samantha has ended up in court. We're just a normal family wanting to lead a normal life. We have had constant grief from the day we moved in. I have had to take time off work to stay with Samantha as she was being tormented whenever I left the house.'

The whole area was being terrorised.

'This gang of kids aged from thirteen to twenty run this estate,' he said. 'Nobody around here will stand up to them for fear of reprisals. Our kids were in tears and terrified to leave the house. They have been traumatised by this. Samantha decided to make a stand and look what she got.'

They had exhausted all legal channels before becoming victims of the law themselves.

'We have complained to the local council and the police but it has not stopped their appalling behaviour,' said Kirk. 'It came to a point where Samantha felt she had suffered enough. Samantha knows she shouldn't have cuffed the three teenagers but you have to understand what she has been through. The legal system is all back to front. They are making out Samantha is the aggressor. It's all wrong. We're now looking to move as soon as possible.'

They had little choice as the terror tactics seemed set to continue. Ms Nicholson had been told by the mother of one of the children that she would be 'sorted out' after the court case.

When 64-year-old retired lab technician Diane Bond stood up to a gang of youths that had been terrorising her, she was both injured and arrested for her pains. For months, a gang of youths some thirty strong and aged eleven to seventeen had been plaguing the local area in Llandrindod Wells, mid-Wales, with an endless stream of vandalism. There was damage to property and cars. They intimidated locals, made a lot of noise and hurled rubbish into people's gardens. Diane Bond complained that they had made her life a misery. They subjected her to foul abuse and barred her way when she was out walking her dog near her home.

Eventually, she snapped when the ringleader, who towered over her, said: 'Come on, old lady, hit me if you dare.'

She prodded him in the stomach. He retaliated by pushing her to the ground and breaking her arm. A few hours later Diane was hauled off to the police station for three hours of questioning under caution. She was finally released at 1.30 a.m. A file of evidence was sent to the Crown Prosecution Service. But after a month's consideration, they decided it was not in the public interest to proceed with the case.

CHAPTER 17
PUNISHMENT SHOOTINGS

The most fertile soil for vigilantes in the UK is Northern Ireland. After more than thirty years of terrorism, faith in the police had been badly damaged and paramilitary groups on both sides of the political and religious divide dispensed summary justice within their own communities. Throughout the Troubles, knee-cappings or summary executions were used by paramilitaries against alleged criminals and as a way of exerting influence. But this was supposed to have ended with the Good Friday Agreement signed in 1998. However, ten years on, Northern Ireland was plunged back into vigilante violence with a rise in the number of death-threats and so-called 'punishment shootings'.

These brutal attacks were carried out by dissident Republicans against anyone they deemed guilty of crime or antisocial behaviour. Vigilante groups tried to take over from the police, imposing a rough justice that was brutal, violent and often arbitrary. However, in Catholic areas where distrust of the police was exploited by the dissidents, there was some support for the vigilantes.

One victim, identified only as Matthew, told the BBC that a punishment squad visited him in his home. One night three masked men burst into their living room and hit him over the head. They told his girlfriend Silvia to get down on the floor with her child. One man held Matthew down, while the other two shot at his legs.

'I thought they were going to shoot him dead,' said Silvia. 'I definitely thought that I was getting shot dead. It was a nightmare.'

Matthew was left with a bullet in his right leg and a bullet hole in the living-room floor. In his early thirties at the time of the attack, he now walks with a pronounced limp, while Silvia and their young son, who saw the whole thing, remain on medication to cope with the fear trauma. The family believed dissident Republicans ordered the attack after Matthew was accused of being a drug-dealer. Matthew denied ever being involved in selling drugs, though he was caught nine years before with a small amount for his own use. Nevertheless, the rumour that he was a dealer spread on the streets.

He said that the dissident Republicans make these attacks 'because they can'.

'They have guns so they can do it and no one's going to say anything about it,' he said. 'If you're going to the police you're getting a death-threat the next day. There's nothing anyone can do.'

The police told him they were working on his case, but were making no progress. He did not hear from them again. Meanwhile, he was intimidated by his assailants, who would regularly drive past his house. He was afraid to report this.

'I don't tell the police anything, because they don't do anything,' he said. 'We're too scared. It's just the way it is. I just can't say nothing.'

This vigilante action has a political dimension. Victims like Matthew and his family are cowed. It increases the gulf between the public and the police, allowing the dissidents to operate with impunity.

During the Troubles, thousands of people were maimed and disabled in punishment shootings. But in the years following the Good Friday Agreement, the number of punishment shootings in both communities fell from a high of nearly 200 a year to just seven. This dramatic reduction led many people to believe that summary justice meted out by the paramilitaries was becoming a thing of the past. However, between April 2008 and April 2009, twenty attacks were reported – eighteen of them in Catholic Nationalist areas. And the rate was increasing. In the first week of April 2009 alone, three men were shot. The Real IRA and the Continuity IRA were thought to have been involved. However, in

Northern Ireland's press, a group calling itself *Óglaigh na hÉireann* – 'Soldiers of Ireland' – claimed responsibility for fifteen of the punishment attacks.

In the midst of it all, Father Martin McGill, parish priest of St Oliver Plunkett Catholic church in west Belfast, commented:

'This parish community, or this area, certainly, has seen a number of so-called punishment beatings and shootings. We've had a few people taken in from other areas, they've been shot here and then afterwards it has emerged that the dissidents have been involved in that.'

However, he said that these vigilante groups inflicting punishment shootings often had the backing of the local community: 'There's an element of that. I would have to say that they will get some sort of support from some people, so that they will be seen as trying to do something "positive" to help the community.'

In parts of west Belfast – as in the rest of the country – people were plagued with a considerable amount of antisocial activity. And there were attacks on the elderly. It took time and effort to get the police to step in and catch those responsible. Then came the long-drawn-out process of taking criminals to court. Even then some of the perpetrators were out on the street again within a short space of time. But where the paramilitaries were involved there were no time-consuming procedures. They dispensed 'instant justice'.

'There's a very strong sense of "it happens here, it

happens now",' said Father McGill. 'People begin to feel "well that makes me feel good, I'm glad to see these ones get their comeuppance".'

This was how justice was meted out during the Troubles by paramilitaries in both the Republican and Loyalist communities. But at that time, normal policing was virtually non-existent in parts of Northern Ireland. Then, ten years on, dissident Republicans began to believe that reinstituting punishment shootings would help them gain popularity.

At the Royal Victoria, the Belfast hospital that receives many of the victims of punishment shootings, David Keeley, a consultant and Clinical Director of Fractures, said that the kneecappings and other injuries to the legs were very similar to the cases he used to see when the Troubles were at their height. The victims were usually young males and handheld low-velocity weapons were used to inflict the damage.

The vigilantes who carried out the punishment shootings were very professional. Describing an attack, the wife of one of the victims said that she knew the armed men who had invaded her home meant business when they put on latex gloves. One man told her to stay in the sitting room and turn the volume on the television up high while the other man took her husband into the kitchen to be shot. The mother of another man in his thirties who suffered a punishment shooting told the BBC that afterwards her son went 'off the rails'. But few victims were willing to speak openly.

There was a protocol to the shootings, with Father Gary Donogan of the Holy Cross monastery in north Belfast sometimes acting as a negotiator. Paramilitaries would contact him, often by phone at the monastery, and issue a threat. He would then contact the individuals concerned and tell them.

'You have to inform them that the threat has been issued,' said Father Donogan. 'If they come to you and confess to you – and I don't mean in the area of Catholicism, I mean in a general statement like, "I will desist from this behaviour and I hold my hands up" – if they give the word and promise to you then the threat will be lifted.'

The organisations that have contacted him included the Real IRA, the Continuity IRA and Óglaigh na hÉireann. He reckoned that he managed to avert as many as two dozen punishment shootings in one six-month period. This was achieved by getting people to make a very public confession of their guilt.

'But the problem with that is, who am I to have that kind of authority?' he said. 'Because, in a sense, it's almost turned me into Caesar. If I put my thumb upwards then the person's OK, if I put my thumb downwards they're not.'

One of the most disturbing aspects of the punishment shootings was that disaffected Republicans – thought to number only about 300 – still had ready access to weapons. And in 2009 they seemed to be gaining ground. Set against them was the organisation Community Restorative Justice Ireland, which was founded in the 1990s with the aim of persuading paramilitaries to stop maiming people in their own communities. Its director, Jim Auld, a former Republican prisoner, also found himself negotiating with gunmen.

'The people that are doing the shooting come from the community,' he said, 'and they know the individuals involved themselves.'

Again there was a strict protocol involved within the dissident organisations.

'Once somebody has reached a particular level, they will take the decision about who is to be shot,' he said.

The decision had to be made high up because the logistics of a punishment shooting were extremely complicated. Once the punishment squad had been instructed, the armourers were called in.

'They will have to go to a house where their guns are stored,' said Auld. 'They remove the guns from the house and bring them to another house where the people who are going to do the shooting collect them.'

Meanwhile, those controlling the action send out their spies.

'They also have the people to monitor where the individual is who's going to be shot,' said Auld. 'They have to get into a situation where they've got control of him, and they have to shoot him.'

It was a risky business.

'At all stages of the process those people are liable to be arrested and either suffer the possibility of getting killed or arrested and put in jail for a very long time,' Auld said. 'However, they believe in a lot of cases that they're doing that on behalf of the community.'

Dissident Republicans plainly believe the benefits of carrying out these punishment attacks outweigh any risks. When they targeted a convicted rapist in April 2009, most local people said that it was not such a bad thing. However, while many in the community support vigilante actions against individual criminals, few support attacks on the state or the police. The dissidents' actions were designed to undermine the police and the state, though. They regard Sinn Féin as traitors to Republicanism for signing the Good Friday Agreement. Then in 2007, when Sinn Féin made a commitment to support the new Police Service of Northern Ireland, hard-line Republicans were outraged.

'In historical terms, and in emotional terms, there is still a major difficulty with policing and what it represents for people in the past,' said Auld. 'There are very few people in this community over 35 who haven't had direct bad experiences with the police – where people have been murdered, tortured, and abused by those same police. So to expect them to flip over and start supporting the police, as anybody else would in a normal society, is too much to ask. I have said before that it would take a generation for that to take place.'

By carrying out punishment shootings, the dissidents were trying to convince people that they, and not the Police Service of Northern Ireland, were protecting the Catholic community from crime. Not only were they dealing with suspected criminals, the shootings in themselves intimidated people. They were consequently afraid to have dealings with the police, rendering the PSNI ineffective. But the Chief Constable, Sir Hugh Orde, remained confident that the PSNI could tackle punishment shootings.

'The numbers of punishment shootings still remain incredibly low compared to seven years ago,' said Sir Hugh in 2009. 'Politically, Republicanism has moved ever more towards supporting and understanding the need for an effective, balanced and proportionate policing service and that's what we're seeing. You have Sinn Féin on the policing board. You have the SDLP on the policing board. You have the Unionists on the policing board, from both the UUP and the DUP. The board represents the community and the boards hold me to account.'

The rise in punishment shootings was a worry to the PSNI.

'We're worried about any crime,' said Sir Hugh, 'and of course punishment shootings indicate clearly some people have not signed up to new dispensation of a new moving-forward, modern Northern Ireland, so we take them all very seriously indeed and they are investigated by my major enquiry teams.'

However, the BBC have pointed out that no charges have been brought in any of the cases of punishment shootings they have investigated.

While expressing his sympathy for the families, Sir Hugh pointed out the difficulties presented in any investigation.

'These are the most difficult crimes to solve simply because of the nature of the crime, the brutality of it and indeed the fact that communities still sometimes don't feel confident in talking to the police service,' he said. 'With everything else in perspective, punishment shootings currently are about so-called vigilante groups trying to deliver a policing response, which they think is appropriate, which is brutal, violent and of course does not work. Punishment shootings has never worked: it is just a brutal and violent response from a very small number of people who are basically thugs. Our job is to catch them.'

In an effort to counter the punishment squads, local community workers have set up a number of projects aimed at building trust between the community and the PSNI. As a result they themselves received death-threats, some from the Continuity IRA.

One of the community workers who received one

identified herself only as Paula. She said that the police told her that she needed to review her own personal safety. 'So I'm assuming that there is a threat to harm me,' she said.

She then had to tell her partner.

'I took him to a public place and told him so he wouldn't crack up in the house,' she said. 'He was exceptionally concerned. I think his attitude is he knows the work that I do, but he never anticipated that it was going to involve a threat because of my doing that work. And certainly he doesn't want me to give up the job, but he does have a reservation when it turns round and affects our safety.'

As a Catholic, it concerned her that dissident Republicans were turning on their own.

'You're seen as a legitimate target if you work with PSNI,' she said. 'But in one part you've got people who really want to try and make it work, in the other part you've got keep them out of the area. And if you keep them out of the area and you report anything, you're targeted. You're seen as an informer.'

But she refused to give in to the vigilantes.

'I can stand up and say, "Look, I'm doing my job",' she said. 'Or I can walk away and they've won.'

Another community worker named Peter, who worked in Brownlow, Craigavon – near where Constable Stephen Carroll was murdered in March 2009 – said that various IRA factions were still recruiting in the area.

He spent most nights patrolling the huge estates between the towns of Lurgan and Portadown and talking to young people there. Behind them, he said, were groups of older people who were pulling their strings.

'Tell me that these thirteen-, fourteen- to seventeen-year-olds can be armed with hundreds of petrol bombs and missiles on a whim,' he said. 'Who organises that? Logistically that is a massive operation. They don't take it from under their beds. This stuff has to come from somewhere.'

In April 2009, two of the three punishment shootings were in Londonderry. On 1 April, 26-year-old taxi-driver Jim 'Busy' Gillespie was watching television at a house in Creggan Heights with his partner and two female companions. At 11.30 p.m., four gunmen burst in. They shot him six times, leaving him with injuries to the legs. A fourteen-year-old boy was in bed upstairs at the time and heard the shooting. The assailants fired a number of shots into the air and three rounds into the victim's car before escaping.

A neighbour who rushed to the scene just after the attack said: 'He was going into shock and the girls were in hysterics. There were bullet holes along the sofa and blood everywhere.'

The victim was a nephew of Patsy Gillespie, who was killed in a bomb attack on the Coshquin border checkpoint in 1990.

On the same day as the taxi-driver's shooting, a 28-year-old man was seized while out walking. He was bundled into a car by four men and taken to the Colinville area of the city where he was shot in both knees and the ankle. Two days before, a convicted sex offender had also been attacked by vigilantes in the city.

Londonderry's two bishops, Seamus Hegarty and Ken Good, condemned the shooting. They described the attack as 'immoral and indefensible', adding: 'The group or individuals responsible had one purpose. It would appear that the motivation is to gain power within their community, to impose control within communities rather than to serve them. It is also indefensible for any group or individual to try to mask their real purposes by claiming to mete out some form of vigilante "justice".'

Meanwhile, a vigilante group calling itself the Bogside Republican Action Group threatened traffic wardens and TV licensing officials.

'As well as shunning them, reasonable people should give us the information to put these vigilantes behind bars, where they belong,' said Chief Inspector Chris Yates.

In Ballymena, four men were arrested and charged with affray, possessing offensive weapons, criminal damage and aggravated burglary. Men armed with sticks and other weapons gathered in the Sandown Park area.

A man was attacked and his arm broken. Cars and flats were attacked. One was set on fire. A crossbow bolt used in the attack was confiscated. The troubles followed the drug-related deaths of two men.

'We cannot have a situation where vigilante mobs are running around deciding who is going to be attacked,' said Ulster Unionist councillor Neil Armstrong.

Vigilantes in south Belfast adopted more traditional methods. They tarred and feathered an alleged drug-dealer when police refused to take action against him. The victim, who was in his thirties, was tied to a lamp-post while masked men poured tar over him and then covered him in feathers as women and children looked on. A sign was put around his neck saying: 'I'm a drug-dealing scumbag.'

'This type of behaviour has no place in a civilised society,' said Margaret Ritchie, Northern Ireland's Social Development Minister.

The humiliating punishment took place in a Loyalist stronghold. But despite the Ulster Defence Association's strong presence in the area, the paramilitary organisation's spokesmen denied any involvement.

Frankie Gallagher of the Ulster Political Research Group claimed: 'The UDA told the local community to go to the police about this. The community responded in the way it did because it had no confidence in the police.'

Meanwhile, a self-styled vigilante group calling itself Parents Against Cocaine and Ecstasy – PACE – warning parents about drug-pushers selling cocaine and ecstasy, was being monitored by the police. They plastered lamp-posts in the Rosetta area of south Belfast with posters warning that drugs were being sold to school-children as young as twelve or thirteen for as little as £1.50. The PSNI were worried that the group might resort to further vigilante activity.

Chief Superintendent Ian McCoy said: 'We would caution any individual or group against taking the law into their own hands. Those who do may themselves commit offences and may subsequently be liable to prosecution.'

Republican vigilantes also operated over the border in the Republic of Ireland. In June 2009, an organisation calling itself Republican Action Against Drugs claimed responsibility for a pipe-bomb attack in the village of Manorcunningham in County Donegal. The bomb had been thrown under a car at around 1.30 in the morning. It was crude but viable, bomb-disposal experts said. A number of people were woken by a loud bang, and a couple and their eight-year-old child were evacuated from their house when the area was sealed off while scene-of-crime officers conducted their investigations.

A few hours later the group phoned a local radio station to claim responsibility. The Gardai in County

CHAPTER 18
THE HAND OF VENGEANCE

At 2.30 a.m. on 1 November 2008, 23-year-old hoodie Donald 'Bones' Donlan was found in a pool of blood in an alleyway in Partington, near Manchester. He had been stabbed repeatedly and kicked in what was thought to be a vigilante attack.

A woman living near the scene said she had heard shouting in the early hours.

'I looked out of the window,' she said. 'There seemed to be a fight going on but I couldn't see much. Groups of teenagers always congregate round there. There's always noise or something going on.'

Donlan was rushed to Trafford General Hospital where he later died. He had been released from jail seven months before for his part in a savage attack on a man and his stepson.

'Donlan was a neighbour from hell, a yob who caused nothing but trouble,' said a Partington resident. 'No one would be surprised if someone decided to get even with him for all the misery he has caused on this estate. His tearaway behaviour has finally caught up with him.'

A long-time thug, Donlan had a criminal record that included actual bodily harm, criminal damage, disorderly behaviour, intimidating a witness, carrying an offensive weapon and robbery.

'Donald was "Jack-the-Lad",' said his aunt Wendy Longbottom. 'He had been in and out of prison but he didn't deserve that. I was there while he was dying.'

Donlan was also thought to have been involved in gang warfare in the area.

'The word on the street is that someone with a score to settle bided their time then picked their moment,' said a resident. 'It looks like his enemies finally caught up with him.'

Chief Superintendent Janette McCormick, who led the murder hunt, said: 'We are working with community leaders to ensure people in the area feel safe. This tragic incident has left Donald's family and the wider community devastated. We are grateful to this close-knit community for its support in our inquiry so far. But we are appealing for anyone with any information around the circumstances surrounding Donald's murder to get in touch with us. We have now put high visibility patrols in place, including community contact points, and we have set up confidential telephone lines. We have been working through the day with community leaders to ensure that people in the area still feel safe, and this will continue. Incidents of this nature are very rare in Partington.'

Donlan left a son Dylan, aged four, by his girlfriend Amy.

'His tearaway behaviour has finally caught up with him,' said a local.

Others were more sympathetic. Friend Jordon-Olivia Gee created a website in his memory.

'Terror at times – but he just used to be a friend from round the corner, that used to pass by day after day saying hello,' she said. 'His cheeky little grin that he used to pull when you knew he did something wrong was so funny. Then it got to the terms when my cousin met with Bones. They were together for quite a while. He used to sleep over at my house with Amy all the time. They would wake up the next morning having breakfast with all of us. He used be so nice with the kids and he was loved so much. Then Amy and Bones had a beautiful little boy called Dylan. He is so cheeky. Aged four now, his cheeky grin is the double of Bones. To find out now that Bones has passed in a terrible way upsets us all. He might have been a rebel to other people but to me and my family he was a top guy that will be missed greatly ...

'Writing this now upsets me but he will always stay in our minds as the cheeky funny man. He will always be missed and when my cousin Dylan grows older we will pass on the things we remember Bones as. If you're wondering how he got his nickname Bones – when he was little he was dead skinny and tall like a skeleton and from then everyone called him Bones.

'For the people who hated Bones, there was twice as many that loved him. R.I.P Mate you will stay in our hearts forever.'

A cousin who also contributed to the site said: 'He used to be so nice with the kids and he was loved so much.' Friends and family left flowers at the scene of the fatal stabbing. Donald's mother Diane Longbottom said: 'Donald was a doting son to me and adored our family, especially the younger children. He told me he loved me every day. He was loving and caring and would do anything for us. He was always there.'

Despite Donlan's violent reputation, the community did not shield his killers. Within days three men had been arrested. Three months later, three women were also charged. In June 2009, 23-year-old Jason McPhee pleaded guilty to the murder of Donald Donlan. Manchester Crown court was told that a group of people shouted and encouraged as he stabbed Donlan twenty-six times in a scene that could have been plucked from a horror movie.

Donlan had been walking home from the house of Chantelle Longbottom, his cousin, when he stopped off at the Partington home of nineteen-year-old Yasmine Bell to cadge a cigarette. McPhee was there along with Yasmine's boyfriend, 22-year-old Ian Brian

Stringer, his 47-year-old father Ian Stringer, his partner 31-year-old Sharon Hughes and their friend 23-year-old Rebecca Flood. They had met up there after their various nights out.

While Donlan was at the house an 'incident' took place, the jury was told. Donlan then returned to his cousin's house on Kent Road to arm himself with a baseball bat belonging to Chantelle's partner Jeffery 'Jay' Fagan. He intended to return to Yasmine Bell's house to confront McPhee.

'From her upstairs window, Chantelle Longbottom saw the deceased leave the house carrying the bat he had been given by Fagan,' said Simon Jackson, QC, prosecuting. 'He appeared to be in pursuit of three men who were at the far end of Kent Road. These men appeared to Chantelle Longbottom to be carrying what looked like knives. She could not identify these men, but she heard the deceased shouting at them as he chased after them. She then heard banging as though the bat was hitting a fence. A short time later she heard the deceased walking back towards her home. He was now being followed by three males. She then saw that the deceased had been surrounded by a group of men and women at the far end of Kent Road, and he appeared to have pushed himself against a metal fence. From her upstairs window, Chantelle Longbottom could see and hear somebody in the group shouting: "Bones, we are going to kill you. You are dead."'

The jury was told that the group included three males – McPhee, Stringer Snr and Stringer Jnr who were leading the confrontation. As Donald swung the bat at the group, one of them dropped a knife to the floor and the group 'surged' towards the deceased as he ran off down an alley.

Jackson told the jury that Chantelle Longbottom 'could hear the pursuing group shouting at the deceased "Bones, you're dead." That was the last time she saw the deceased alive. She then heard the deceased respond by shouting: "Put your knives down and I will fight you all one on one." That was the last she heard of the deceased.'

The court was told that others had seen Donlan being chased down the alleyway by the group led by McPhee. Witnesses described seeing three females at the scene. Flood had sent a text message to her friend Thomas Graham saying that Jason and Ian were in trouble.

Graham then phoned Flood to see what was going on and she told him that they were fighting Bones. The court heard that Graham, his girlfriend Laura Phillips and their friend Kyle Ferguson – who was also a friend of the deceased – arrived at Middle Lane, Partington, to see Donald running away from his attackers.

'As the events unfolded, Thomas Graham saw the three female defendants standing by and watching the continuing attack on the deceased,' said Jackson. 'Sharon Hughes was laughing and in a happy mood.

The other two girls looked scared, but Thomas Graham sensed they knew what was going to happen. The Crown's case is that the female defendants were not mere spectators – they were involved in the murder of the deceased, in that they were encouraging the male defendants in their attacks on the deceased, with shouts of "he deserves to die" – this as Laura Phillips later tried to intervene and stop the attack. Indeed, Yasmine Bell came up to Laura Phillips when she arrived. She was "upset and crying" and said to Laura Phillips: "I don't know what to do. I've kicked him in the head."'

According to Jackson: 'This admission by Yasmine Bell, of participation in a continuing attack on the deceased, evidences her direct involvement in this murder, beyond encouragement and vocal support that was given by Sharon Hughes and Rebecca Flood, to one of actual participation in the murder. It is plain that the deceased had been followed, attacked and stabbed even before these witnesses arrived on the scene.'

Bell, Hughes and Flood denied murder.

The jury was told that McPhee was shouting threats of 'I'm gonna get you. I'm gonna kill you' while waving a large kitchen knife. While Kyle Ferguson tried to help Donlan, who was hiding behind a garden fence, the court was told that Sharon Hughes said: 'Come on, he's down here.' Donlan was then subjected to a savage and brutal attack by McPhee, who was on drugs at the time.

Donlan was stabbed and slashed twenty-six times,

and stamped on by McPhee. The jury was told that Stringer Jnr and Stringer Snr were standing on each side of Bones encouraging McPhee to continue the stabbing. They also prevented Ferguson from stopping the attack.

The jury was told that Stringer Jnr said to McPhee at one point, 'I need to do my little bit,' before kicking his victim in the stomach, punching him and then stamping on his head.

Jackson added: 'The Stringers' physical support, and Sharon Hughes' vocal support, submits the Crown, makes them guilty of the deceased's murder – even though they never wielded the blade which killed him.'

In her statement to the police, Laura Phillips described the attack as being 'like something from a horror movie'. The court heard she could hear the knife cutting the defendant's skin and was almost sick at the scene.

The jury was told: 'So severe had been the attack that witnesses could only make out the victim's eyes by seeing the whites of them, due to his head and face being covered in mud.'

The three women, Sharon Hughes, Yasmine Bell and Rebecca Flood, were found not guilty on the directions of the judge. The Stringers, father and son, denied murder but were found guilty after a long trial.

The same week that Donlan died, twenty-year-old Dwayne Ayres from Yateley was stabbed to death in a suspected revenge killing days after he was released early from a two and a half year sentence for causing the deaths of two teenage friends when driving dangerously while high on drugs. At 2 a.m. on Sunday 2 November 2008, a gang burst into a house where he was staying in Hook, Hampshire. They dragged him outside and knifed him repeatedly. After the attack, the fatally wounded Ayres was taken by car to Frimley Park Hospital in Surrey where he died at 3.50 a.m. A post-mortem examination carried out by Home Office pathologist Hugh White at the Royal Hampshire County Hospital in Winchester confirmed Ayres died of a stab wound.

Relatives and friends laid flowers outside the house where he had been killed. A card on flowers left by his mother Vanessa read: 'Dwayne, I don't know what I'm going to do without you. You were always my sanity and strength. I love you so much always.'

A second card said: 'A light from our lives has been taken, no farewell words spoken in our hearts, memories of you live on, from Granny and Grandad, Auntie Helen and Dave.'

In a statement released through police, his family said he would be missed by his partner Emily and their eighteen-month-old son Richard.

'Dwayne was a lovely, caring son to Vanessa and will be greatly missed by all those who knew him for what he was and will always be remembered for,' the statement went on. 'He had just started to live his new life with his love Emily and their son Richard. The family and the large extended family of relatives and friends will miss Dwayne and we would ask everyone to respect their privacy at this time of tragedy.'

Ayres had been jailed in October 2007 at Winchester Crown court for causing the death of his friends, fifteen-year-old Callum Forbes and eighteen-year-old John Bryant. The teenagers were passengers in a Peugeot 206 being driven by Ayres that hit a tree outside a school in March 2007 after he lost control driving at 66 mph in a 40 mph zone.

The court was told that Ayres had driven the wrong way around roundabouts – as well as overtaking on blind bends, narrowly missing oncoming traffic. Two other passengers were injured and Ayres suffered a punctured lung. Blood taken from Ayres, then nineteen, confirmed he had taken cocaine shortly before the crash.

After Ayres' trial, Sergeant Spencer Wragg of Hampshire Police said: 'Dwayne Ayres had a total disregard for any other road user on that day. Lots of parents had started gathering outside the school waiting to collect their children when the crash occurred, and it is a miracle that no other members of the public were killed or seriously injured. His actions led to the death of two of his friends and that is something he is going to have to live with.'

Diana Forbes, the mother of Callum who was killed in the accident, said she expressed grief over Ayres' death.

'I am really saddened and shocked to hear the news about Dwayne,' she said. 'It is a great tragedy. I do know that he was trying so hard to rebuild his life and support his young family. My heart goes out to all his family and friends.' With her husband Rob, she added: 'We miss our wonderful, beautiful, charismatic son.'

Bryant's parents Lucy and Adam said after the sentencing last year: 'Whatever happens will not bring our son back. We would not wish this on any parent.'

The bungalow where Ayres was attacked was understood to be rented to a group of about four young men in their late teens or early twenties. It was thought that Ayres was staying there, rather than with his family in Church Crookham, near Fleet, to avoid being found.

A neighbour said it was feared he had been targeted due to the fatal crash.

'About two weeks ago there was another incident at the same house when the door was kicked in,' the man said. 'It sounds as if someone was looking for Dwayne to settle a score – possibly over the deaths of the two boys. He'd only just come out of prison after serving his sentence, now this has happened.'

Another neighbour said: 'There was a fight there a

few days ago. All of this must be linked, it's usually a very quiet, normal road.'

The £175,000 whitewashed bungalow where Ayers was killed stands on tree-lined Holt Way in a residential estate populated by families and retired couples.

One resident said: 'There are a few young lads that live there but they've only been in for a few months. We don't know them at all.'

Another neighbour said: 'I don't know if he was staying there in the hope no one would find him after coming out of prison – but it seems likely.'

Local people said they were puzzled that Ayres' friends drove him thirteen miles to Frimley Park Hospital near Camberley, Surrey, rather than the North Hampshire Hospital in Basingstoke, which is just six miles away.

Detective Superintendent Kevin Walton said: 'This is an unusual and isolated event and we have specially trained police officers out in the area to help us establish what happened.'

Forensic officers examined the scene of the attack and a second house nearby was also cordoned off and searched by specialist teams. Soon after, six people were arrested on suspicion of murder and three others on suspicion of aggravated burglary.

'We will not be drawn on the specifics behind the motives of this attack,' said Detective Chief Inspector

Colin Mathews, 'particularly as a number of people are in custody.'

In another victim-turned-vigilante tale, 34-year-old Gary Parkin, of Saltwell Place, Gateshead, became an armed avenger after two men had robbed him at knife-point. After reporting the attack to the police, he went home, armed himself with a fourteen-inch carving knife and went hunting for his assailants. However, his plan backfired when his search took him to a convenience store that his prey had robbed. He was grabbed by the police who suspected him of robbing the store – the very crime committed by the men he was pursuing. Although he was cleared of involvement in that offence, he was charged with carrying an offensive weapon.

'He said he felt like a ninja sniper pursuing the offenders and said that his purpose was to apprehend them and cause them some injury,' said prosecutor Sue Barker.

He told police that he was a 'peaceful person', but that 'anyone would do the same thing if they were subjected to an attack'.

Parkin pleaded guilty and was given a four-month prison sentence suspended for a year. Magistrates said they had considered sending him to prison but had been swayed by his personal circumstances. The court heard that Parkin was an alcoholic who turned to drink because he could not cope with the death of his mother eighteen months before and had attempted suicide nine times. He was given a supervision order for a year that would require him to undergo treatment for his alcohol dependency.

In the wake of the 2008 banking crisis, an anti-capitalist group calling itself Bank Bosses are Criminals made a vigilante attack on the home of Sir Fred Goodwin, the disgraced former chief executive of the Royal Bank of Scotland. After bringing the bank close to collapse, he took early retirement with a massively inflated pension. The police were alerted when an alarm went off at 4.30 a.m. on 24 March 2009. Three downstairs windows had been broken at Sir Fred's Edinburgh home. A black Mercedes was also damaged in the attack. Neighbours had not seen anyone at the house for some time. Sir Fred's children had been taken out of their private schools and it was thought they had gone abroad. The organisation warned of further action against similar targets. They seemed to have some support. There had been protests outside the house for some time, after it emerged that Sir Fred had negotiated a £16.9 million pension package which he said he had no intention of paying back. Banners outside his Edinburgh home condemned him as a 'scumbag millionaire' – a sardonic reference to the Oscar-winning movie *Slumdog Millionaire*. The morning after the vigilante attack, one protester told reporters outside the house that the best course of action would be to 'burn it to the ground'.

CHAPTER 19
THE NATIONAL
VIGILANTE ORGANISATION

Although most vigilante action is taken by local people dealing with local problems, in the UK there is a National Vigilante Organisation that set up its Navigor website in 2006. This takes particular delight in ridiculing Tony Blair's old mantra: 'Tough on crime, tough on the causes of crime'.

The Navigor site complains that the victims of crime have been betrayed for years by incompetent ministers and a police force which cares more about political correctness than actually catching criminals.

'Today the government has totally abandoned the fight against crime, ordering the police and the courts to stop sending criminals to jail, allowing them instead to go on terrorising innocent communities,' it says.

The organisation protests that those attacked by criminals are arrested while the criminals walk away, and those who try to defend themselves risk going to jail for assault. The number of drug-related crimes increases daily, it says. Children attack and murder each other. Successive Home Secretaries have been incompetent and the only thing the government does is tell lies, saying that they are reducing crime rates. The only thing you can do about it, the Navigor site insists, is join the National Vigilante Organisation.

Although Tony Blair resigned on 27 June 2007, Navigor reserves most of its opprobrium for him. It even says: 'This website is Tony Blair's REAL legacy – dedicated to fighting the thugs and scum HE didn't have the guts to!'

It talks of Blair's 'ten-year betrayal' and says: 'In a free, civilised society with proper laws designed for the PROTECTION of all honest people, there should be no place for a vigilante organisation. But we no longer live in such a society – we live in a society which is exactly the opposite – where the laws have been corrupted so they no longer protect the innocent but the guilty – and where the innocent are now persecuted by the very legal system which should protect them!'

It insists that the police no longer care about justice and have become merely the pawns of their political paymasters. The only thing decent people can do if they wish to live in a decent society again is to become vigilantes.

The site also tells the tale of men like David Orchard who helped police catch criminals for almost twenty years with closed-circuit TV cameras he installed at an unmanned rural train station he had bought in 1991 at Adisham, Kent, to convert to a three-bedroom property.

He spent some £25,000 on CCTV equipment – the newest can email photographs of criminal activity to the police. His footage helped capture vandals, trespassers and car thieves. It also alerted authorities to children risking their lives by running or cycling down tracks where trains pass at 60 mph and the live rail carries 750 volts.

However, when Govia took over the south-eastern train service in the spring of 2006, he was told his services were no longer needed, so Orchard pulled the plug on his fifteen CCTV cameras. Nevertheless, when he saw people committing crime, such as starting a costly fire in a nearby shelter, he called the British Transport Police to report it. Eventually, the police got fed up with his complaints and took him to court.

'Even though I had taken my cameras down, I still felt like I had a responsibility to report worrying incidents to the police,' he said. 'Obviously they now see me as the nuisance, so apparently I am supposed to ignore anything bad that appears to be happening even though it's right on my doorstep.'

Then there was the case of Mohammed Shafiq who got a call from his son Umar, an A-level student, saying that he was being surrounded by youths in a park near his college. The boy had been beaten up before and had been the victim of a lengthy campaign of bullying by a gang at Burnley College, so Shafiq immediately rang the police. He then drove to the park. This took fifteen minutes, but when he arrived the police had still not turned up, even though the police station was only half a mile away.

In front of fifty onlookers, Shafiq tried to calm the situation down. But when he tried to protect his son, the attackers turned on him. He was hit over the head with a metal bar and stabbed in the stomach. He died in hospital seven hours later.

In another case Navigor highlights, 42-year-old mother-of-two Denise Chapman was told by the police to take vigilante action when her £4,500 horse trailer was stolen – even though they knew exactly where it was from the moment it went missing. Chapman had received a call from a woman rider who saw the trailer being taken from the stable yard where it was parked in Reigate, Surrey, so she phoned the police. The witness followed the thieves on to the M25 before a male rider at the stables picked up the trail. From there, the trailer was driven east into Kent before heading through the Dartford Tunnel into Essex.

Chapman stayed in touch by phone and the Surrey Police notified each force as it entered their area. After an hour, the trailer disappeared into a travellers' site at Basildon and the friend dared go no further.

'Essex Police suggested that I go to the site and

contact them when I'd located the trailer and they would then meet me there,' she said. 'I am a mother of five-year-old twins who I'd have to have taken with me. To expect me to go unassisted to a gypsy site on a dark night beggars belief.'

The site also highlights the farcical aspects of modern police – the ban on jokes on a newsagent's leaflets in Wales in case they were offensive, policemen being sent on health and safety seminars to teach them how to climb three feet up a ladder to install anti-speeding devices, fifty officers turning up to arrest a twelve-year-old boy who had found ten pounds in an ATM machine, while gangs of youths armed with sticks, spades and screwdrivers fought it out on the streets of east London in a battle that lasted twenty minutes – and the police did not even turn up.

Navigor opposes the introduction of identity cards on the grounds that they will criminalise ordinary citizens without improving security or catching illegal immigrants. It, predictably, backs the return of capital punishment. The website also carries a page called 'Nonce Watch'. This attacks a judge and policemen seen to be lenient on paedophiles and warns of the danger of a government database of children that could be a 'paedophiles' paradise'. It also names sex offenders thought to present particular danger to the public.

Tony Blair's justice minister Lord Falconer, the Home Office, the Human Rights Act and the 'PC brigade' are all selected for particular opprobrium. Would-be vigilantes are urged to fight back via the worldwide web.

'By using the internet we can change public opinion, and more importantly, make certain that the failures of the Government and the various agencies who should be protecting us are made public,' Navigor says.

CHAPTER 20
CRACKING DOWN
ON THE GOOD GUYS

Mrs Dunn, a 66-year-old grandmother, thought she was doing the community a good turn as she cleared unsightly junk from the plot of land. Instead, she was dubbed a vigilante. She had spent days removing the rubbish, including a mass of weeds, a broken washing line and an upturned shed, only to receive a letter from the local council, telling her to stop immediately.

Retired gardener Mrs Dunn has kept her own allotment in Sherborne, Dorset, in good order for twenty-five years and could no longer bear to look at the untidy neighbouring plot which had been left to go to rack and ruin.

'The site looked so bad after two years of nothing and it was starting to encroach onto my allotment so I decided to do something about it,' she said. 'I cleared and dug half of the plot but had to stop because I couldn't lift the heavy stuff like two dumped fridges.'

So she wrote to the council telling them what she had done. She asked them politely to get the person who had rented the plot to clear the rest of it – or clear it themselves.

'They wrote back saying I had taken vigilante action and I must desist immediately,' she said. 'I find that very offensive. We all help people at the allotment and for them to turn round and say I am a vigilante indicates he doesn't live in the real world. There's just no way I am a vigilante and I took great umbrage at that.'

Mrs Dunn then turned her guns on Sherborne town council, who eventually made a formal apology. The problem, they explained, was that they were trying to get the tenant of the unkempt allotment to give it up as they were not taking care of it and Mrs Dunn's efforts to tidy it up was not helping their case.

Another guerrilla gardener set about improving the environment in Standish, near Wigan, even if it meant breaking the law. Graphic designer David Rourke took it into his own hands to clear the litter and plant seedlings in the land surrounding the disused Standish railway line.

'Technically, I suppose, if the land is owned, what I'm doing is illegal,' he said. 'But if the land is uncared for and is public access land, and there doesn't seem to be any activity from anyone else, then why not? If

I break the law in the name of improving our area then it's a risk I'm prepared to take.'

The self-styled 'Longbridge Vigilante', 83-year-old John Hotchkiss, also fell foul of his local council. For eight years he had been painting out vandals' graffiti on a long wall in his neighbourhood.

'When I first started people said, "You'll never beat these kids, you know." And they were probably right,' he said. 'But I kept going week after week, month after month, year after year, until finally the idiots got the message that it was no good tagging that particular wall because within a few hours it would be back to a pristine condition.'

Then the council covered the top of the wall with anti-vandal paint. It was a thick, gooey, tar-like substance designed to prevent vandals climbing over it. Instead, it gave them a whole new medium.

'The taggers couldn't believe their eyes,' said Hotchkiss. 'They didn't have to buy a spray-can, marker-pen or crayon as everything they needed was there.'

They simply took handfuls of the tar and daubed it over the wall.

'Unfortunately for me it was too thick to dry so I couldn't paint it out,' Hotchkiss said.

The council was blissfully unaware of the problem, but said it would launch an investigation.

*

Another vigilante wall-cleaner struck in Arbroath. This time a well-intentioned member of the public who took it upon himself to clean graffiti from the wall of Arbroath Abbey may have done more harm than good.

Over Christmas 2008, the word 'Kay' appeared in letters three feet high on the wall of the Abbey's Regality Tower, and it was feared they would be costly to remove. However, a retired Arbroath man, who had returned home from overseas for the holiday, took matters into his own hands when he suspected that the silver letters were not paint, but merely a decorative festive spray.

'When I looked closely at the writing, it didn't seem like paint to me,' he said. 'So I licked my finger and applied it to a bit of the lettering – which promptly vanished.'

Grabbing a bucket of soapy water from a nearby shop, he removed the rest of the graffiti. But a negative image of the graffiti later returned. This required expert removal. Historic Scotland urged people to contact experts rather than undertake work themselves.

The vigilante dog-walker who was attacking cyclists in a Colchester park may have been civic-minded, but he had to be stopped. The town council received four separate reports of people being shoved from their bikes as they rode in Castle Park. In each case a pedestrian – a man accompanied by a large dog – physically pushed the cyclist off their bike while they were in motion. None of them had been seriously injured, but it was feared that both pedestrian and cyclists might be in danger were the vigilante action not stopped.

Bob Penny, parks and recreation manager for the council, said: 'There was an accident a few weeks ago in the park following a conflict between a dog and a cyclist and that appears to have started this.'

Ian Baalham, parks and recreation officer for the council, said the council was working closely with other agencies to try to stop the rogue dog-walker.

'We have been working with police to try and catch the person,' he explained. 'If people are cycling through the path, where it is clearly signposted "no cycling", then they should not be doing that. However, we do not condone this person's actions. He is taking the law into his own hands and it is unacceptable. We have been working with the police, street wardens and park rangers to try and clamp down on cyclists riding through the park and more importantly, to catch this man and take appropriate action against him.'

In December 2008 vigilantes smeared dog mess on the door handles of cars owned by Capita workers who parked their cars in a residential street in Bishop's Cleeve, Gloucestershire.

'Something has to be done,' said a resident. 'Some Capita workers are parking illegally and blocking junctions. The police don't seem to do anything – they come out and look but don't do anything.'

Then there is the Cleethorpes Vigilante Inshore Lifeboat Service, founded in the 1960s after a group of young riders lost their lives on the beach there. More recently they renamed themselves Cleethorpes Rescue to sever any association with lynch mobs.

Vigilante Kenneth Wilson, 62, was trying to defend this planet from alien invasion when he was arrested. However, the intergalactic intruders he sought to keep at bay were a group of Norwegian crop-circle enthusiasts who had come to see the latest 300-foot creation in a field near Devizes in Wiltshire. The trespassers allege that he fired a number of warning shots before he was halted by an all-too-readily identified flying object – a police helicopter.

The ufologists had come to inspect the crop-circle, thought to represent a bird with its beak open, when they said Wilson opened fire and ordered them to get off the land.

'The gunman was dressed in full camouflage garments, had a black mask over his face and held a gun in his hands,' said 47-year-old Eva-Marie Brekkesbo. 'When I asked him if he was the farmer, he said that he was engaged by the farmer to prevent anyone from visiting the crop-circle. I have been visiting crop-circles for a decade and have in various ways been told that we are not welcome, but this is the first time I have been threatened with a gun. Farmers have the right to protect their land, but they have no legal right to threaten people. It was totally unnecessary and incredibly scary.'

One of the group called the police and with the help of an observation helicopter that was in the area officers swooped in to nab the gunman at around 2 p.m. on 14 July 2009. He was later released on bail.

But the owner of the field, farmer Richard Oram, claims that there was an entirely innocent explanation. Kenneth Wilson had simply been shooting at pigeons with his 64-year-old brother Sid.

'Sid is ex-firearms,' Oram said. 'He's always shooting pigeons and rabbits on our farm. He and his brother both had permission to be there.' The creation of the circle, which appeared on 9 July, would have disturbed the land. This would have kicked up a large number of insects and seed that would have attracted plenty of birds. However, he admitted that crop-circles are a problem for him.

'This one alone will have caused £1,000+ damage,' he said.

Another worker at the farm near Devizes described the crop-circle as vandalism.

'If people go nosing around on other people's land they are trespassing and will be removed,' he said.

Expert Steve Alexander, who spotted the crop-circle

when flying overhead, said: 'I have never encountered anything like this before. We know crop-circles are man-made and they cause huge problems for farmers because these crops are grown to earn the farmer income. However, there is no justification in using a firearm to intimidate people – that is simply illegal and totally wrong.'

But if the police cannot protect crops from man-made criminal damage, farmers may be tempted to take the law into their own hands.